The Art of the Pendulum

The Art of the Pendulum

Cassandra Eason

Boston, MA/York Beach, ME

This edition first published in 2005 by
Red Wheel/Weiser, LLC
York Beach, ME
With offices at:
368 Congress Street
Boston, MA 02210
www.redwheelweiser.com

Library of Congress Cataloging-in-Publication Data
Eason, Cassandra.
The art of the pendulum / Cassandra Eason.
p. cm.
Includes bibliographical references and index.
ISBN 1-57863-356-7
1. Radiesthesia. 2. Pendulum. 3. Dowsing. I. Title.

BF1628.3.E22 2005
133.3'23--dc22

2004065050

TCP
Printed in Canada

12 11 10 09 08 07 06 05
8 7 6 5 4 3 2 1

Contents

Introduction

A pendulum – whether an elaborately carved crystal on a silver chain or a key on a piece of string – is one of the easiest ways of accessing the intuitive powers we all possess, but may find hard to trust. By tuning yourself into the way a pendulum swings you can dowse for water or make decisions about your life and relationships. In the area of health, a pendulum amplifies healing energies from the natural world and can dispel negativity. And the pendulum is so portable that you can use it almost anywhere as a wise guide to set you on the right path or assure you that your present course, whether emotional or physical, is correct.

What is Pendulum Dowsing?

Dowsing or rhabdomancy, sometimes known as divining or water witching, is an ancient practice in many cultures whereby hidden water, minerals or oil deep in the ground are detected by the means of the movements of a forked stick held between the hands. Pendulum dowsing, using a weight on a chain, dates back hundreds rather than thousands of years, but has become increasingly popular because it offers a finely tuned method of dowsing. The pendulum is usually favoured over rods or a forked stick for answering questions, locating lost objects by dowsing over a map, choosing lucky numbers and finding ghosts.

The pendulum can be regarded as a receiver and transmitter of information, although the source of its knowledge is the subject of endless speculation, ranging from angelic guides to our own subconscious that is able to pick up cues not accessible to the conscious mind. Despite the fact that its power is scarcely understood, the pendulum is increasingly used even by military organisations. For example, US marines were taught to use pendulums in Vietnam to locate land mines and underground tunnels.

There is no doubt that the sixth sense plays a part, because the information received does involve knowledge beyond the five senses, certainly in their accepted form. However, it may be that as with animals, human senses do extend far beyond their recognised physical limits and that by practising dowsing it is possible to tap these hidden powers. We have all felt danger in the pit of our stomachs or detected the sense of a peaceful presence in a place, and it may be that the pendulum is expressing these physical/psychic sensations through a form of telekinesis that causes the hand to make an involuntary muscular response. It is sometimes said that the pendulum, or indeed any other dowsing instrument, brings together the rational and intuitive faculties, the left and right sides of the brain, and enables you to make informed decisions using all potential sources.

It is possible to learn to dowse without using a pendulum, however the instrument is a confirmation of the inner insights and, what is more, acts as protection when dowsing for the unknown or in sensitive areas – a touchstone when charting unfamiliar territory (see chapter 2).

Choosing Your Pendulum

A pendulum is usually defined as a symmetrical non-magnetic weighted object, centrally suspended from a single light chain or cord. But in practice you can dowse with almost anything, as long as it is sufficiently solid so as not to be blown about by the wind if you are dowsing outdoors. Some pendulums have a hole in the side for a 'witness', for example a fragment of the material being sought or in the case of a lost animal, one of its hairs. Alternatively, this material can be attached to the pendulum or carried in the other hand, although a tangible focus is not imperative.

Your chosen pendulum can be a conventional long crystal quartz rounded or pointed at one end that contains living energies of the earth, although some dowsers prefer to use rose quartz or amethyst if the quest concerns decisions about feelings or life changes; you may decide to have two or three pendulums for different purposes. Smaller crystals or wooden weights of a diamond shape that can be specially purchased attached to a chain are also popular divinatory tools, or you may choose to create your own pendulum with a trinket, a ball made of metal (even a Chinese medicine ball), a key, a glass bead, a brass nut or a plumb bob from the local DIY shop, any of which can be attached to a cord or a piece of string, if necessary using wire or a metal cradle around the object.

In its simplest form you can improvise with a key tied to a shoe lace, or a heavy curtain ring or plain gold ring attached to a pencil with a length of cotton wound around it and secured with a paper clip, both of which can be instantly constructed when you need a pendulum in a hurry and have left yours at home. The master dowser Tom Lethbridge once claimed to have successfully dowsed with a piece of chewing gum on a thread. If you do adapt an item of personal significance, such as a pendant or a special ring, you may find that the positive emotions attached to it help you to tune into your intuition.

Holding Your Pendulum

The string is held between the thumb and forefinger, however there are two diametrically opposed views as to which hand should be used. The first suggests that you should use the hand with which you write, sometimes called your power hand, winding any extra chain around the index finger of the same hand; the other view suggests that it is better to dowse with the left hand for right brain intuition. The old question 'how long is a piece of string?' applies here, and indeed was probably first used in connection with dowsing, for recommended string lengths vary between 27cm (9in) and 120cm (40in). Especially while you are familiarising yourself with the technique, the string should be fairly short, and if you are dowsing over a chart or map, 15–20cm seems most successful. You can wrap any excess string or chain around your index finger. Different lengths seem to work for different situations and you may find that for physical outdoor dowsing somewhere around 45cm (15in) works well. Simply experiment until you are so at ease with your pendulum that it becomes an extension of your arm.

Can Anyone Dowse?

As with many intuitive arts, children are natural dowsers and many successful adult dowsers began in childhood before doubts and inhibitions arose. My daughter Miranda, who is 13 at the time of writing, is an expert dowser and will happily play games of hunting hidden objects with the pendulum.

The American Society of Dowsers says that everyone is born with the ability to dowse, and that in any group of 25 adults, between two and five will obtain the dowsing reaction immediately – others may have to practise for a while before they become confident dowsers. The problem with adults is not that they cannot dowse, but they think or fear that they cannot do it and so block the inherent ability.

Some dowsers are happy to undertake tests, however the majority of people work best in response to an actual need, especially where emotion is involved, rather than in an artificially structured situation. So if a decision matters to you, it will be easier to obtain an accurate response from the pendulum.

The Forces Behind Dowsing

This book concentrates mainly on using a pendulum, but the theories put forward hold true for all forms of dowsing. Attempted scientific explanations have varied over the centuries with new discoveries, but all seem to stumble on an unknown factor linked with the human psyche.

Early explanations interpreted dowsing as signals from the auras of underground water or metal. This was followed by theories of a sympathetic attraction between specific minerals and rods cut from certain trees. Some people still believe that substances such as flowing water, oil or gold emit a strong natural energy and that the divining tool acts as an aerial which picks up these vibrations and transmits them to the dowser. However, this does not explain how some dowsers can successfully locate oil or water by holding a divining tool over a map of an area. Can there be a symbolic link between the map – the symbol – and the dowser?

Magnetic or electrical influences on dowsers and their rods were also considered a viable rationale for a time, only recently being replaced by theories that the source is radiation or waves akin to the electromagnetic waves emitted by television or radio stations.

Can it be that the pendulum has a mind of its own? Certainly the pendulum is what most people describe as an inanimate object. Yet craftsmen who spend their lives shaping inanimate objects will talk quite seriously of materials that have a life of their own: pieces of wood that are calling out to be made into certain objects; blocks of stone that have statues inside them waiting to be freed.

Psychologists also speak of anthropomorphism, and suggest that we are increasingly returning to primitive thought forms, whereby we supply inanimate objects like cars and boats with a personality. If we do indeed psychically endow objects with a personality, this could be one explanation for the dowsing rod with a mind of its own.

Another is that our higher consciousness, a benign spirit or angelic guide, directs the pendulum or other divining tool. Divination traditionally meant getting in touch with a 'divus' or god for inspired direction for a future course of action. This controlling force may be easier to accept if it is regarded as the 'divus' or god within, the Higher or Evolved Self inside us all, the Wise One whose knowledge is drawn from a pool of the experience of mankind in all places, past, present and future.

Often we impose unnecessary limits when we try to break down paranormal phenomena into single entities, for example telepathy, precognition, clairvoyance and clairsentience. All of these practices are involved in dowsing at different times, and as you work with your pendulum you will find that in other aspects of your life your innate intuitive powers develop automatically.

Since all diviners work best in one specific area, I have included research from a variety of sources so that the book can lead to a competence far beyond my own. As this is primarily an introductory guide, I have also given other sources of information and societies should you wish to develop your own expertise either generally or in one particular direction.

Types of Dowsing

Pendulum dowsing can be used in many different ways and spontaneously taps the basic human ability to be drawn to what it needs. But it is important to remember that pendulum dowsing is an art and not a science, and if you do try to rationalise or devise a series of tests each time you ask a question, you are blocking the flow of unconscious power with conscious doubts. The main forms of pendulum divination are:

Dowsing for natural underground substances: such as water, oil or gold. Their physical vibrations may strike a resonance with some instinctive force within us that causes the pendulum to move, in the same way that we feel peace or dread in certain places as actual bodily sensations. This form of dowsing is the most difficult to demonstrate, because unless we need to find drinking water, the emotional aspect may be quite weak and the expectations of others quite high, so that anxiety may intrude. For this reason, this may be an aspect of dowsing better left until you are more confident (see chapter 9).

Dowsing for decisions: Here, a flow or options chart can be created as a guide through even the most complex decisions. It may be a case of the unconscious nudging the divining tool and can be explained by telekinetic forces – our unconscious is able to weigh up the pros more accurately than our conscious which is often clouded by wishful thinking or the opinions of others. For many people this is the most accessible area of pendulum work and one I have often demonstrated on television to sceptical presenters who have then felt the pull of the pendulum. The validity of the demonstration is verified by a viewer at home carrying out the process simultaneously and independently. This method works even if I am using the pendulum on behalf of a person hundreds of miles away and the matter concerns health, love, business, happiness or prosperity.

Dowsing for earth energies: According to the theories of feng shui and geomancy there are lines of energy which run through the earth which can be beneficial or harmful. We can use the divining tool to seek these out and rearrange our homes or workplaces to make the best of these forces or neutralise them where necessary.

Dowsing for health: This can be divided into sections:

☆ dowsing for the root of illness by passing a pendulum over the body to find the area that needs treatment. This can also be used with chart dowsing and can pinpoint quite unexpected sources of pains and allergies

☆ dowsing for a remedy – using the pendulum to find out which of a selection of potentially appropriate herbs or medicines might best alleviate the problem

☆ preventive dowsing – using the divining tool to ask the question: 'Is this substance good for my health?'

Dowsing for lost objects: such as car keys and wallets. If the lost items are your own or belong to family members the search energies are amplified by your emotional associations with the objects and the places you have driven in the car using the keys, and by the overriding need to find the item. Or it may be that your unconscious is slowly remembering where you put them and is guiding you by invisibly nudging the pendulum or dowsing rod. It is possible to use this method for objects lost by others if you can tune into the emotions of those who have lost them. Lost pets can also be found by this means, assuming the pet wants to be discovered.

Dowsing and psychic phenomena: You can successfully see or sense ghosts by tuning into the places they walked, especially during periods of intense emotion, or contact spirits at sacred sites or along ley lines. In my own experience of pendulum ghost hunting, it is the feelings of people in times past imprinted at a specific place where a tragedy or intensely happy event occurred that causes the pendulum to register.

My Own Interest in Dowsing

I have used a pendulum for years for making decisions and for health matters, and in 1994 wrote a book called *Pendulum Divination for Today's Woman* (Foulsham) in which I put together what I had discovered about the intuitive processes involved in dowsing. At about the same time, on a visit to Scotland, I was introduced to pendulum dowsing for ley lines by an expert but very open-minded and patient diviner

John Plowman, who managed to fill me with enthusiasm for the subject on a muddy day near Loch Lomond. John's own mathematical research into the links between ley lines, dowsing and ghosts is described in my book *Ghost Encounters* (Blandford, 1997). More recently I have explored the fascinating connection between legends of giants, witches or fairies and the strong ley energies that can be detected with a pendulum in the places where these myths have grown up.

Although I have regularly divined for lost animals and objects with some success, until recently I have avoided water divining and dowsing rods, possibly because the idea has never excited me. However, while making a TV programme in Hampshire a water diviner demonstrated his technique and I used hazel and metal rods to detect underground streams. This helped me to realise that the divisions I had placed between this and other kinds of divining were artificial, once I trusted and relaxed into my intuition and relied on the same methods of visualisation while dowsing that worked so well in other aspects of pendulum divination.

Water witching started me on a whole new study of black streams or lines of energy. They may help you to live more harmoniously whether at home or in a work environment, and so avoid the physical/psychic stresses that can lower your resistance to disease. This brought together both my earlier earth energy explorations and dowsing for health.

EXERCISE: CHARGING A CRYSTAL OR METAL PENDULUM WITH POWER

☆ To charge the pendulum, circle it with amethyst, rose quartz and clear quartz crystals and place in running water until the water is full of bubbles. You can use a clear glass or Pyrex bowl held under a running tap, or use sparkling mineral water from a siphon, that will already be aerated.

☆ Put a few grains of sea salt into the water and stir it with your power hand (the hand you write with) nine times, to activate the ancient elements of Earth and Water, saying: *Earth and Water, endow with wisdom and intuition my pendulum, that I may hear the gentle, inspired counsel that comes from my heart and from my ancestors and descendants as yet unborn.*

☆ Remove the pendulum and leave it to dry on a circle of gold foil in the sunlight from dawn to dusk on a clear day to absorb Fire and Air power, the ancient elements that were believed to make up all life and together created the fifth element, Ether.

☆ As dusk falls, light a pure white candle and pass your pendulum nine times through the flame, saying: *Candle of Fire, burning in Air, give clarity and accuracy to my pendulum that it may speak the truth as it is and not as I would wish to hear it.*

☆ Leave the candle burning in a safe place so that the light falls on the pendulum, and when it is burned through place your pendulum in dark silk or a small black velvet bag until you need it.

☆ Recharge your pendulum whenever you feel it is necessary or after you have encountered negativity.

1

The History of Dowsing

Cave drawings provide evidence that dowsing was practised from the earliest times, and it would seem likely that these early dowsers were looking for water from an underground source. Such veins sometimes form pools within cave structures and it may be that the dowsers were the arbiters of suitable cave dwellings, where the water gushed through the rock offering a source of water for both drinking and washing. These subterranean pools were sometimes dedicated to the Mother Goddess and regarded, like sacred wells, as the water of her womb. One such drawing of a man with a forked stick in his hands was discovered in the Tassilin-Ajjer Mountains in east central Algeria and has been carbon dated to around 6000 BC.

The Chinese and Ancient Egyptians also practised the art, especially in the search for precious metals and gems, as shown by illustrations on pottery, paintings and papyri.

The first mention of a dowsing rod in literature is in a 1540 publication on mining, *De Re Metallica* by Georgius Agricola, at a time when there was a great interest in alchemy and all things magical. Several academic theses on the subject followed in the subsequent centuries, among which J.H. Martius's *De Virgula Divinatris* is one of the most famous. Even in these early times, doubts were raised as to the validity of this method of divination. An early sceptic commented: '[Dowsing rods] be meer toys to mock Apes, and have no commendable device [purpose]' (Reginald Scot, *The Discoverie of Witchcraft*, 1584).

Books on dowsing were among the first to be printed in the 16th century, and in these as well as on old coins of the period the dowser is seen at work with his forked stick. In the Bergbau Museum at Bochum, Germany, there is an 18th-century Meissen figurine of a dowser in the uniform of a miner.

Rowan dowsing rods, cut from the magical tree of protection, have been used over the centuries for detecting metals, and the hazel rod, a wood associated with wisdom, is still traditionally the choice for divining for water and buried treasure. This link with trees accords with my own favoured origin of the term dowsing rod, from the old Cornish 'dewsys' (Goddess) and 'rhodl' (tree branch). However the second and more traditional view roots it in the Middle English derivation, 'duschen' meaning 'to strike', from early German references to dowsing rods striking down towards the ground.

A form of dowsing for decisions, one of the most popular uses of pendulum dowsing in the modern world, was first recorded in the 1st century AD when Marcellinus, a Roman writer, described a tripod from which hung a ring on a thread. On the circumference of the tripod was a circle showing the letters of the Roman alphabet and the ring spontaneously swung towards different letters to spell out answers to divinatory questions. That this practice persisted into the Middle Ages is indicated by a Papal bull issued by

Pope John XII in 1326 forbidding the practice of the 'use of a ring to obtain answers in the manner of the Devil'. A description also survives from 1553 of a peasant suspending a ring on a thread over a half-filled container of water and using this for dowsing.

The most famous female dowser was probably Lady Milbanke who so annoyed her son-in-law, the poet Lord Byron, with her hobby that he wrote after her death: 'She is at last gone to a place where she can no longer dowse.' Was this because she dowsed to discover his indiscretions . . . ?

Dowsing also journeyed with the colonists to the US and to Australia and South Africa and proved a valuable method of locating existing wells and sources of water for their settlements.

Until Victorian times, therefore, dowsing was a natural art and one which was the subject of much experimentation. But because it was inexplicable in terms of material science dowsing was marginalised, and with the growth of urban life with its municipal water systems, one of the main practical applications of dowsing fell into disuse except in rural areas.

The Revival of Dowsing

But dowsing refused to die, and from time to time remarkable examples of its power emerged to trouble those who sought to dismiss it as superstition. In 1913 a report by a French biologist, Vire, to the Academy of Sciences, described how a network of catacombs dug under Paris since Roman times had been pinpointed with seemingly inexplicable accuracy by a group of dowsers working on the surface.

Indeed, after the Second World War, expansion in suburban building and the rebuilding of bombed cities once more brought the talents of the water diviner to the fore, as conventional and expensive methods of locating water frequently proved inadequate.

During the 1960s the American dowser Verne Cameron was asked by the government of South Africa to help them to locate the country's valuable natural resources, in particular minerals, using his pendulum. However the US government would not allow him to leave the country as his dowsing abilities had already marked him as a security risk in the eyes of the CIA. His 'crime' was that in 1959 Cameron successfully located on a map every submarine in the US Navy plus every Russian submarine in the world using his pendulum. He also identified all the submarines in the Pacific Ocean on a particular day, distinguishing merely from the map which belonged to the US, which to Russia, and those from other countries.

In recent years, dowsers have been employed by oil and pharmaceutical companies, as well as governments, sometimes secretly but more increasingly quite openly. What is more, even military personnel are recognising the ability of dowsers to detect enemy tunnels, and to find unexploded shells on land and mines at sea.

It may be that as pendulums and other divining tools enter the everyday sphere, their powers are accepted as a tangible expression of our innate intuitive powers, so that these quite natural abilities are no longer regarded as weird or nonsense and can be utilised as they were by our ancestors in every area of life.

2

Beginning Pendulum Dowsing

Discovering Your Pendulum's Responses

Once you have chosen your pendulum – or it has chosen you – and you have charged it psychically, you need to discover the unique way in which you and your pendulum interact and to programme it to give information in specific situations.

☆ Carry your pendulum with you in a small velvet bag or wrapped in silk in a purse or pouch so that it will not become scratched, and spend a few minutes each evening sitting quietly in candle light, allowing your pendulum to move gently without asking it questions or seeking information, so that it becomes an extension of your psyche.

☆ Empty your mind of all conscious thoughts, worries or even questions. To help this process, visualise a crystal jug of pure water being poured gently into a fast-flowing stream; or imagine a star-studded sky, then let the stars disappear one by one until only the velvet night is left; or play soft music based on natural sounds (see Useful Addresses for sources of suggested music). This conscious emptiness is the perfect state for allowing your unconscious wisdom to be expressed through the pendulum. If it does not come naturally, let the ability unfold over time.

A 'Yes' Response

Frequently a clockwise circle or ellipse forms the 'Yes' response, and this response remains consistent once established, whether the pendulum is used for questions about health, happiness or money, or for tracking water, lost objects or even ghosts.

Since our emotions are a trigger and a channel for successful pendulum divination, to find your personal 'Yes' response visualise a very happy moment, a success or a peak experience. It may be the time when you suddenly mastered a skill or reached the top of a high mountain, either in reality or symbolically, and felt an overwhelming surge of joy. The pendulum will respond to the recalled positive emotion with a 'Yes' response.

A 'No' Response

A negative pendulum movement is generally the mirror image of the 'Yes' response, for example, an anti-clockwise circle or ellipse, however your own pendulum's 'No' may be entirely different. Discover this by concentrating on a moment when you were disappointed or failed to reach the peak of your particular mountain and, as you momentarily recall your sadness, your pendulum will move on its 'No' path. Follow this rapidly with another happy recollection and your pendulum will express positivity once more.

The 'Ask Again' Response

Sometimes the question you consciously formulate is not the issue that really concerns you on a deeper level, or it may be ambiguously phrased. In this case your pendulum may simply cease to move, or circle first one way then the other. This is usually a sign to rephrase the question or to try a completely different approach.

Identify this important signal by holding your pendulum and thinking of a time of confusion, perhaps when you caught the wrong train or lost your way in a strange town. Your pendulum should then demonstrate this vital movement.

The Neutral Position

As a general rule, if you are following a trail with your pendulum, the pendulum may swing freely in the neutral position until you approach the target when it will give the positive response. If you go off-course, the pendulum will make a negative response to warn you and will return to the neutral swing when you are back on track.

However, some people have discovered that their pendulums adopt the positive response all the time they are on-course; the closer to the target, the more enthusiastic the swing becomes, rather like a dog straining at the leash (see chapter 4).

Testing the Responses

On the whole it is easier to test and practise your different pendulum responses in real-life situations rather than by asking questions to which you already know the answer, although this method is sometimes recommended for getting to know your pendulum. Before beginning, you should always ask your pendulum either silently or out loud whether it is the right time to dowse. If the answer is negative, wait for a while, as there may be too much clutter in your mind to enable your pendulum to answer the question accurately; it may also be that the question cannot be dealt with at this particular time, perhaps because other people are so closely involved that their actions or reactions are dictating the course of events. A neutral response may indicate that you should wait before making any decisions.

Listen to your subconscious, and it will guide you via your pendulum if you do not try to anticipate or rationalise its information. It has been said that the best dowsers work on the 'parcel principle' – the question in their minds is always: 'I wonder what is in that parcel?' – a state of open anticipation that does not try to second-guess or analyse in advance the contents of the message.

The more definite the pendulum's response as measured by the size and vigour of its circling or as powerful vibrations in your fingers, the more clearly the answer is either affirmative or negative. A less certain answer, a 'Yes But', is not an indication that the process is not working properly, but rather may invite further questions or a wider area of search.

Asking the Right Questions

The technique for asking the pendulum questions is similar to that of using a computer. Both have immense data bases and resources to tackle almost any issue, but both depend on human input – *you* activate the computer and pendulum.

As with the computer each of your questions should be phrased to exclude any possible ambiguities. In the case of the pendulum a 'Yes' or 'No' response should answer the question or resolve a dilemma, so questions cannot be open-ended or have qualifications. This is not as easy as it sounds. You cannot ask for options or opinions beyond those phrased as 'should I/can I/will I?'.

It is also difficult to get accurate answers about the intentions of others, and can be regarded as a no-go area in terms of free will and privacy. Some dowsers will even ask the pendulum if a lost animal or person wishes to be found before embarking on a search and it is important to steer clear of areas where intervention – psychic or otherwise – is unwelcome.

You may decide to write down the question or to speak it out loud (see chapter 3). Either way, create clear parameters; you may need a series of questions to eliminate various factors. For example, if you are asking a question concerning your diet you might begin with: 'Should I eat this biscuit at this point in time?' If the answer is 'No', you may then wish to establish whether the particular kind of biscuit is the problem, as it may be that you have an allergy to that brand of biscuit. If not, you might next ask whether it was the wrong time, for example you have not long finished a meal and are not really hungry, merely bored.

Once you have exhausted this line of inquiry, your subsequent questioning could include whether biscuits generally may be an unsuitable food for you, either because they trigger a food binge or contain an ingredient common to virtually all biscuits and indeed other similar foods that may also cause problems, for example are you intolerant to fats or sugar?

So from a simple inquiry you can examine quite complex issues, especially if you use a flow chart (see chapter 3) and ask a series of sub-questions for each point.

Creating a Time/Intensity Chart

You can use a time/intensity chart to establish a timescale or grade a response. Create a circle using a clock face marked in the appropriate number of divisions. Although it is a common practice to create a number strip or arc, the pendulum operates naturally in circles and I have found that the circle method is most effective. Keep a series of circles ready

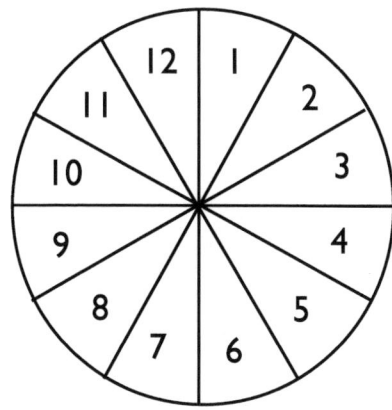

A time chart with 12 divisions which could be used to represent months or five-minute intervals

to mark out. You may also like to keep a journal of your results over a period of time.

The divisions within the circle will vary according to the question you are asking; the question: 'In how many months' time will so-and-so occur', would require 12 divisions and so on. There are no limits to the areas you can tackle using this method, for example you could ask: 'How many minutes late will my bus be?' using perhaps five-minute divisions as on a normal clock face. In such an instance, be specific as to the number of the bus, train or airline carrier and route. For questions of degree or intensity, one to ten is a workable gradation, for example 'On a scale of ten how good will this herb be for me right now?'. If you are trying to assess the depth of underground water you can again use multiples of ten as necessary.

Psychic Protection

With all psychic work, you need to protect yourself from the negative feelings of others that may be projected, whether consciously or unconsciously, towards you. This is especially important if you are using your pendulum to ask questions on behalf of other people who may be carrying negativity in the form of their worries, or if you are operating where there are powerful energies, for example on ley lines or at sites of great antiquity, or if you are dowsing for ghosts, even if these are entirely positive.

☆ Before you begin your first pendulum explorations, hold your charged pendulum towards the sun or to a source of light until it is filled with radiance. Modern optic fibre lamps are very effective as they reflect rainbow colours in gentle spiralling patterns, using the same circular movement along which pendulums operate.

☆ Breathing in very slowly and gently, absorb the light source reflected in the pendulum and exhale the darker rays you visualise. Visualise the light extending so that it encloses you in an impenetrable sphere.

☆ As you create this cocoon of light, think of a power word or action so that you can summon your protective sphere of light rapidly if you suddenly sense free-floating negativity or a hostile feeling directed towards you. For example, you might say: 'When I brush back my hair, I call all my golden protection into being.'

☆ Gradually let the light fade, but be aware of a lingering faint glow all around you.

☆ Call up the protection for your pendulum or any psychic work. Picture the light fading whenever you have finished.

☆ If you are dowsing for decisions in the evening or on a dark day, light a single tall white candle and invoke in the glow your own protective guardian, whether an angelic being, a spirit guide, your own Evolved Self or an undifferentiated form of light and goodness.

☆ Direct all questions to and interpret information via the pendulum especially when working with other people or in places of great psychic power. This way any overly strong or negative energies will be deflected.

☆ Frequently cleanse and recharge the pendulum after intense use.

Recharging Your Crystal

To cleanse and recharge your crystal when it seems to be losing its power or looks dull and feels heavy, run it under water, let it dry naturally and wrap it in dark silk with a rose quartz or amethyst, stones of healing, being careful that they do not come into direct contact with it and scratch it.

An Alternative Pendulum Response

If you are dowsing over a chart for an option, choosing the correct remedy, or gauging timing or the intensity of a reaction on a chart, you may find that rather than giving a positive/negative response over the appropriate choice, the pendulum pulls down or feels heavy. This is the easiest and most instant pendulum response to detect physically. If you are uncertain about your abilities to distinguish and interpret a pendulum's movements, walk over an area where an object has been lost or scribble a number of options on a piece of paper and pass your pendulum across it, asking your crystal to pull down or become heavy when it reaches the correct answer or place.

Once you have experienced this strong sensation, which will vibrate pleasantly through your fingers, the more conventional positive/negative responses follow naturally. The 'This One' movement, although not traditionally sought by dowsers, is nevertheless extremely valuable especially when you are helping others to make decisions using your pendulum, as it is so readily distinguishable.

EXERCISE: TRUSTING YOUR OPTIONS

☆ When visiting a garden centre, hold your pendulum over three unfamiliar pots of herbs or flowers without reading the labels.

☆ Buy the one that your pendulum chooses, either by a positive movement or by pulling downwards. This may not necessarily be the most green and lush plant, but has some intangible potential that is identifiable on a non-physical level. Successful gardeners tend to be very intuitive.

☆ Take it home, and without consulting the label on the best position for the plant offer the pendulum the choice of three or more areas of garden: shady, sunny, with stony or rich soil.

☆ Use window boxes or ledges facing different directions if you do not have a garden.

☆ Plant your herb or plant in the chosen spot and endow the plant with a secret wish so that it is linked to you by positive emotion.

☆ Rely on the pendulum to tell you how much water to give the plant and when to offer it by setting up containers with different amounts of water and dowsing over them, using a circle chart to establish the best watering times.

☆ As the herb or flower thrives, you will have a reminder that making a choice and carrying it through matters more than trying to prove your powers to yourself or anyone else.

3

Dowsing for Decisions

The fact that the pendulum movement is controlled by muscular response is seen by sceptics as a weakness in dowsing for decisions, for it is claimed that the dowser is using the pendulum to confirm a choice he or she has already made. However, unless somone is cheating, which destroys the whole point of the exercise, the hand movement is unconscious and often gives an unexpected result. The principle is the same as that underlying the picking of certain Tarot cards apparently at random from a shuffled pack. In each case, the most appropriate card or correct pendulum response is triggered by psychokinesis (movement of physical objects by mind-power), a process rooted in the unconscious wisdom of the questioner.

Whether we are accessing what the psychologist Jung called mankind's collective unconscious outside conventional definitions of time/space limitations, or touching our personal, deep inner wisdom, there is no doubt that dowsing for decisions operates with an accuracy equal to the more demonstrable forms of dowsing for water or minerals.

Because it is so strongly linked into the personal psyche and usually with the feelings that prompted you to ask the question, dowsing for personal decisions is a form that is instantly successful with many people.

Practice does make perfect in that you learn to ask the right questions from the start, and most importantly learn to trust the wisdom revealed through your pendulum. The pendulum can be very helpful in confirming on the material plane what you glimpsed on the psychic level, as revealed in dreams or sudden flashes of inspiration. The test of time usually confirms the rightness of decisions, and though you would not base major decisions entirely on one pendulum reading, this intuitive output can shed light on logic and expertise and sometimes provide the missing piece in the jigsaw.

While divinatory pendulum readings are best done for yourself, you can help others to make decisions.

☆ Let the person for whom you are reading hold the pendulum and think of a happy/sad/confusing moment in order to establish personal 'Yes/No/Ask Again' responses. These can be established quite quickly and this initial period gives the questioner an opportunity to tune into the pendulum and to imprint personal vibrations.

☆ Ask a question yourself, or get the person for whom you are reading to ask a question, that will prompt a 'Yes/No' reaction from the pendulum.

☆ If it is your own reading, let your mind go blank using the jug of water or the starry sky technique described in chapter 2. This gives your psyche space to work, and if you hold the pendulum in a static position it will begin to move after a pause. Let the pendulum take its time; dowsing for decisions is not a process to be hurried.

☆ If it is not your question, describe the starry sky to the questioner and let him or her relax until the pendulum is ready to respond.

☆ If the question does prompt the 'Ask Again' response, let the rephrased question come spontaneously without the conscious restrictions that may have clouded the original question.

Single Questions

Sometimes a single question can provide the answer to an option or dilemma. It will need to be phrased so that yes or no can be the answer, which precludes the use of either/or within the question. With practice, even quite complex issues can be answered using a carefully phrased proposal. There is no limit to the areas that can be tackled, with the proviso that it should be a question that needs answering and which evokes some degree of emotion in you or the questioner, whether positive or negative.

Using a Flow Chart

An issue may not be not clear cut or may have several facets. The first question may only be a surface aspect of a deeper matter. Using a flow chart and asking six or seven questions spontaneously may suggest solutions that had eluded you, but now suddenly seem the only possible course. Again, you can use this method for another person and you can record the different questions and answers.

☆ Choose a time when you are not in a hurry and will not be interrupted.

☆ Ask a question, this time without consciously formulating it. You may be surprised at your choice, and the 'Ask Again' response that will occur when your question is ambiguous will alert you to blind alleys or circular thinking that may have held you back.

☆ Write the first question at the top of the flow chart, then, as before, blot out conscious thought and wait for the pendulum to speak in its own time.

☆ Record the response in the appropriate column. If the pendulum tells you to 'Ask Again', write a new question in the central column.

☆ If it answers 'Yes' or 'No', write your next question in the appropriate box.

☆ Let the second question also come spontaneously. You may find that the direction is changing or a seemingly unrelated issue comes to the fore. Trust the wisdom of the pendulum and the matter will become clearer.

☆ Continue until you have five or six questions and answers and can see a way forward.

☆ Alternatively, list your questions and write the response next to each question, to form a single column.

A Sample Flow Chart Reading

Suzanna, a divorcee in her mid-thirties, is studying music and has become deeply involved with Tim, one of her tutors who is in his early fifties. Tim is married with teenage children, but has asked Suzanna to travel round the provinces with him at the end of the year in the regional orchestra of which he has just become director. However, he says that he does not want any more children and must remain closely involved with his family until they are grown up, although he wants to marry Suzanna when his divorce comes through. Suzanna has no children and is desperate to become a mother before she is too old.

QUESTION: SHOULD I GO WITH TIM WHEN HE TAKES UP HIS NEW POST?

Not surprisingly the pendulum's response is a definite 'Ask Again', for several different, though related, issues are bound up in this question. Should Suzanna sell her flat in London and give up her part-time career with a magazine that has offered her full-time work in the arts section when she obtains her degree in music? Should she remain in London and spend weekends, holidays and part of the week with Tim so that they can develop the relationship at a slower pace, since Tim still goes home some weekends to be with the children? If she did not join the orchestra, would the distance weaken or strengthen their love? If things went wrong could she re-establish herself in London?

The answer to the last question on Suzanna's flow chart was 'No' because Suzanna acknowledged that Tim had not even mentioned divorce to his wife for fear of upsetting the children. The children were also a major stumbling block if Suzanna could not accept that she would not have a baby of her own and that parenthood was a stage of life she and Tim could not share. However, she did acknowledge that she did not want to give Tim up and so decided to rent out her flat in London for a few months and take unpaid leave from her work. This way they could live together in a fresh environment and hopefully resolve the obstacles to lasting happiness through time, patience and tolerance on both sides.

YES	ASK AGAIN	NO
	Will I regret giving up my chance of having children of my own if I commit myself fully to Tim?	
If I became pregnant, would Tim change his mind about children?		
		Do I resent Tim's close involvement with his children?
	Do I fear Tim cares for his wife and children more than me?	
Do I want to give Tim up?		
		Should I wait until Tim instigates a divorce before fully committing myself?
Will a new life together overcome the present obstacles to happiness?		

A sample flow chart reading

The Grid Method

If you have to make a choice between several options, the grid method is an accurate way of discovering the relative merits of different paths. You may be able to achieve this with a single grid or you may need to draw a series of grids and gradually narrow down information within more detailed parameters until you get a specific answer. With this method you can plan many major life changes.

The Sacred Grid of Nine is an ancient Scandinavian magical device used by wise women and frequently drawn in the earth in front of their huts. In more formal magic situations it was created on a specially erected platform as a protective magical area: the nine squares are contained within a larger protective square, which also concentrates the energies of time and space. The grid formation is especially good for any practical matters, such as finance, business, moving house or travel. For love and relationships, some people prefer to use the circle method – described in chapter 2. Divide the circle into the appropriate number of options, name each and dowse over them as I describe below. However, the grid method can be used quite effectively for emotional and health matters.

☆ Formulate an initial question or area in which there are several options. The options can be represented by one word or be as detailed as you wish.

☆ You may not need all nine squares of the grid, in which case place the options at random within a number of squares; you can ask the pendulum to show you which of the squares to use by holding it over each section in turn and asking it to make a positive response over those you should use for dowsing. If it has selected one segment too few, ask yourself which option is either repetitive or not an option at all. Likewise, if there are too many segments indicated, your pendulum is telling you that you have forgotten an option.

☆ Block off the remaining squares in black or red.

☆ Hold the pendulum 8–10cm above the paper on which you have drawn the squares.

☆ Pass your pendulum over each row in turn, beginning in the bottom left square and moving from left to right in a continuous movement.

☆ Travel right to left over row two and finally left to right over row three.

☆ You may instantly feel a definite downward pull over one square, but see if the pendulum will continue. If it does not, you have arrived at your answer.

☆ The pendulum may hover over two or three squares, as if uncertain. There may be more than one likely option and you may end up combining or reconciling two courses.

☆ If no definite choice has been made, move backwards from top right over the three rows, holding the pendulum firmly until it locks into one.

Choosing a Holiday Destination

If you want to go on holiday but are not certain where, begin by selecting four or five possible destinations. When you have made a selection using logic, your pendulum/psyche may select the one you least favoured consciously. There are places to which you are instinctively drawn even though the choice runs against the logical arguments, but when you arrive you will find the hidden reasons that drew you.

☆ Read as much as possible about the different destinations so that your psyche can make an informed decision, and then write the place names on squares on the grid, blocking off any surplus squares. You might like to scribble a few brief words of description for each destination and then allow your mind to go blank.

☆ When your pendulum has selected an area, you can next read about alternative resorts in that region, selecting five or six that seem suitable. Again, scribble a few notes about each on a second grid and dowse without focusing on them.

☆ When the pendulum has selected a resort, choose nine hotels, apartment blocks or even campsites. Include some slightly beyond your price range; I have found that the *right* accommodation will sometimes be reduced on the day you book or an alternative cheaper date will be offered that on reflection suits as well. You can cut out pictures from the brochures and place them in the squares or write the names on the grid.

Moving House

If you are planning to move house but are not quite sure about where you want to go, you can use the flow chart method to ask a series of questions. Alternatively, if you have a number of areas in mind, put in the research beforehand

and narrow these down to four or five that are suitable. You can do this by stages, first by towns and then by districts or villages. Then use the grid formation to decide on the best area through your pendulum psyche.

☆ When you have decided upon the district or village, read through the literature and narrow down your choice of houses to nine that you think are worth visiting.

☆ Cut out the photographs of these houses from estate agents' material and place them on a grid formation, or you may prefer to write the names of each house and scribble notes.

☆ Pass your pendulum over the grid before viewing the houses. You should then visit them all, leaving until near the end the one or more favoured by the pendulum. Your subconscious may have picked up information the conscious mind missed, especially if you were subjected to a great deal of hard sell.

☆ Run the pendulum over the grid again after the visit and see if the favoured property has changed. Usually the choice remains constant unless your unconscious radar detected problems not visible to the physical eye. This does not mean that the house is wrong for you, rather that you should return – if possible dowsing with your pendulum if you get the chance to be alone. You should also have an extra-careful survey, as it may be possible to resolve any difficulties. The combination of reason and intuition, knowledge acquired from physical exploration, research and from the pendulum, provide a whole picture.

The Hawthorns, Sandy Lane Huge patio, no garage but car space	2 Chiselam Lane Extra bedrooms in loft, near main road but well screened	Peacehaven, Holly Lane Near nature reserve, small garden
24 The Pines Rural outlook, old-fashioned kitchen	103 Loughton Lane Close to main-line station	Ringwood, Love Lane Big garage, but dark bathroom
The Croft, Birchill Road Very modern, but overlooked	188 Wilmington Lane Plenty of character and space, but needs modernisation	Squirrels Leap, Laurel Avenue Lovely garden backing on to woodland, small interior

A sample grid using house names

EXERCISE: CHOOSING LUCKY NUMBERS

We all have lucky numbers that may have become associated with good fortune because of a house number at which we were especially lucky, a car registration that became empowered by our happiness associated with driving the vehicle, a birth date or significant day when we met a partner for the first time, got married or had a child.

No lucky number method is guaranteed to win the lottery, however, for magic is not about huge personal gain. Many practitioners, myself included, find that they can do magic for others but not for themselves — which explains why, although I teach money spells that have worked for many people over several years, I am still hovering on the edge of overdraft.

That said, *you* may be the one who uses the pendulum method and scoops the jackpot first time on the lottery, roulette or even the football pools. What is more, if you do need to decide on a lucky day for an interview, a date, or want to win a raffle in which there is a special prize, then you can dowse over the chart shown, keeping to the range of numbers you need, for example 1–49 for the UK lottery, 1–30/31 for the day of the month, 1–12 for the month.

☆ When dowsing for numbers you need as few preconceptions as possible, so before you begin spend time clearing your mind of clutter. One effective method is to imagine all the numbers from 100 down to 1 printed in black on separate pages on a pure white pad.

☆ Imagine ripping the sheets off one at a time, naming each number in its descending order, visualising the sheets flying away in the breeze.

☆ Tell your pendulum the parameters in advance, for example: 'I need six lucky numbers between 1 and 29' or 'a date in a particular month' (specify 28, 29, 30 or 31 days) or 'a month from 1–12 with January as 1 and December as 12'.

☆ If you need larger numbers, draw a quick chart like the one illustrated overleaf (it can be bigger or smaller according to your needs).

☆ Hold your pendulum over each number in turn and it will pull down or make a positive response over the appropriate numbers.

	2	3	4	5	6	7	8	9	10
11	12	13	14	15	16	17	18	19	20
21	22	23	24	25	26	27	28	29	30
31	32	33	34	35	36	37	38	39	40
41	42	43	44	45	46	47	48	49	50
51	52	53	54	55	56	57	58	59	60
61	62	63	64	65	66	67	68	69	70
71	72	73	74	75	76	77	78	79	80
81	82	83	84	85	86	87	88	89	90
91	92	93	94	95	96	97	98	99	100

A number chart

☆ Keep a record of these numbers, especially of lucky dates, and as you score successes your confidence will improve along with your accurate scoring. If, as a result, you do hit the big one, send me a postcard from your exotic location!

4

Finding
What is Lost

Many people prefer to develop the skill of dowsing for lost objects in real-life situations and not through tests for objects that are deliberately hidden; an actual need and the emotion attached to the missing item help to establish a telepathic connection rather like a homing device, even with inanimate objects. However, if you do enjoy testing your abilities, I have suggested some activities later in the chapter.

For direction hunting you will need a small compass. You can use separate small bags for your pendulum, compass, pens and paper and slot them into a larger bag in which you can also keep a Landranger Ordanance Survey map of a specific area. The bag should be waterproof if possible for outdoor searches and have a long strap so you can wear it on your back or over your shoulder to leave your hands free.

A Direction Chart

A direction chart consists only of a very simple line drawing giving the four cardinal compass points (north, east, south

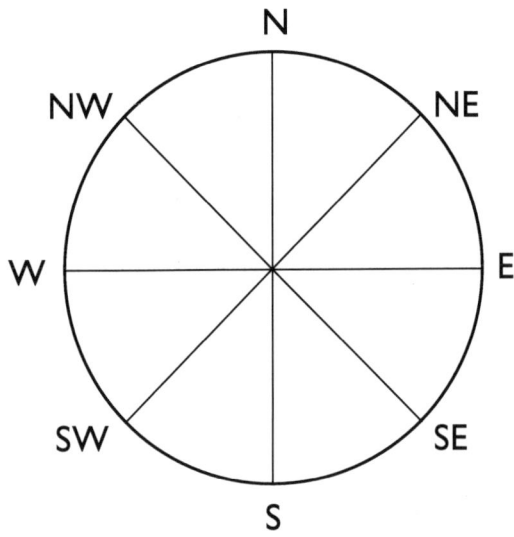

A simple direction finder

and west) and the midway points (north-east, south-east, and so on).

Draw your own chart on stiff card and, if possible, laminate it so that it can easily travel with you as part of your basic pendulum kit. In an emergency, you can scribble an approximate chart on a piece of paper and use it with a makeshift pendulum. Make the chart large enough so that when you hold the pendulum over it, you can clearly differentiate between the directions of the swing.

Using the Chart

This method is very effective because you can use your direction plan absolutely anywhere and can refer to it to keep you on track and alert you to changes in direction on your search.

☆ Define the lost object or pet as specifically as possible; it may help to recite the details out loud. As you do so, visualise the missing item and evoke any associated sounds and fragrances and positive memories of holding or using the object or petting the animal. You can thereby establish a strong telepathic signal. Some people use a sample, for example of a missing pet's hair, either held in the free hand or in the special witness hole that exists for this purpose in some commercially purchased pendulums.

☆ Use your compass to align your direction finder chart to magnetic north.

☆ Hold your pendulum over the direction finder at the central point where the north/south axis crosses the west/east axis.

☆ Ask the pendulum to: 'Show me on the chart the direction in which I should begin my search for . . .'

☆ Beginning in the north, move your pendulum slowly clockwise round the plan. At the right direction, it will either make a small, positive circling movement or pull downwards.

☆ Proceed in that direction, or as closely as you can allowing for any obstacles, until your pendulum stops swinging in its neutral mode or giving your personal positive response if that is its on-course travelling indicator. The pendulum will not be fazed by stairs or obstacles, so when it stops you should stop and ask it to: 'Show me the direction I must next follow to reach the object.'

☆ Place the chart on a flat surface and again return the pendulum to the north/south axis, realigned with your compass, and allow the pendulum to indicate the new direction.

☆ As you move closer to the article, the neutral swing or your positive response should become more vigorous.

☆ The positive movement or vibration will become very powerful to let you know that you are at the right location.

☆ If the pendulum stops and refuses to give a new direction, having made the initial positive response or downward tugging, the object may be out of view and you should look in drawers and under or even behind furniture, checking gaps where the article may have become lodged.

☆ If you are searching for an animal using this method, call out your pet's name and if there is a shed or garage nearby, gain access – the animal may be asleep or frightened. I found one of my cats by dowsing; she was asleep in a summer house the owners insisted had not been opened for months. Again, check drawers and apparently inaccessible spots as cats especially will sleep anywhere.

Refining the Technique for Small Objects

When looking for jewellery or keys in a wide open space, or a document in a series of files or folders, you can programme your pendulum to alert you when you reach your target or inadvertently go beyond it, as you could easily miss the item by looking a few centimetres in the wrong direction. Before you begin, say to the pendulum: 'Just before I reach the object I am seeking, make an ellipse. When you are over the spot where the missing item is, give me a strong positive response and make a reverse ellipse if I pass it.'

To look for a letter or document that you have tidied away, spread out your files in a row and walk by them, asking the pendulum to indicate when you have reached the correct folder. Then arrange all the papers in that file in a row and repeat the procedure. This technique can also be useful if you have put something in a drawer and cannot recall which one. (See chapter 8 for creating a house plan.)

Testing Your Psychic Powers of Detection

Although I prefer dowsing in situations where an actual need exists as I believe this sharpens the psychic senses, I know that others enjoy improving their skills by practising in test situations so that when a real need arises, they feel confident in their abilities.

Standardising the Tests

If you want to practise finding a series of objects which have been hidden by someone else, you will need a number of similar items, for example coins that have no particular individual characteristics that may cause the concealer to register one more than another and so give it stronger vibes that may cause you to miss the others.

For the same reason, choose a fairly uniform location, for example a wood or field with bushes so that the concealer is not especially aware of the individual hiding places. If the items are not valuable it will not matter if in early experiments you do not find them all. Both of the above points avoid the concealer unintentionally communicating the locations.

☆ Before they are hidden, hold the objects in your cupped hands and visualise how you will use them once you have found them.

☆ If they are coins, picture yourself spending them on a treat that will give you pleasure. If you are concealing sweets or small soaps, choose your favourites, so that they are associated with pleasure. Thus you are injecting the experiment with the personal link between seeker and sought that is one of the keys to real-life dowsing.

☆ Go to a place which should not be familiar and certainly not hold any emotional significance that might interfere with the link between you and the items through the pendulum. Keep away when they are being hidden and do not consciously think about the experiment.

☆ As you are seeking several items, the direction chart method will not be helpful.

☆ Stand in the centre of the area and begin walking in ever-increasing clockwise circles.

☆ Alternatively, walk south to north then south again over a widening area.

☆ Ask the pendulum to take you to the first coin by the nearest practical route, i.e. not through brambles.

☆ Visualise the objects as tiny golden lights, like points on an electricity grid.

☆ Continue moving until you pick up a trail, then follow it.

☆ Once you have found the first object, place it in your pocket or hold it in your other hand as an amplifier, and ask your pendulum to show you the best practical route to the nearest object hidden close to your present spot.

☆ Again circle until you are on-course and continue until you have found all the items or no longer want to continue – the point at which to stop even if some have not been found.

☆ You can pick up the trail the next day or abandon the search and use a different set of items on another occasion.

☆ The key to such tests is not to rely on logic or try to work out from the first find the route taken by the concealer. Once you start to deduce, you will block your intuition.

Psi-Tracks

It is believed that the song lines of the Australian Aborigines – tracks that are only marked by references to landmarks such as a natural rock sculpture or rock painting within a song or legend – can guide travellers across thousands of miles. These invisible psychic trails are called 'psi-tracks' and are strengthened each time the song is recalled. In 1987, the Swede Göte Andersson gave this phenomenon its name and defined it as an energy field, created by visualisation, extending between a person and the object on which he or she is concentrating. This has exciting implications for dowsing lost objects, because once the trail is created by the person who lost the object, the track remains in the same place although the original visualiser is no longer present. If the object is moved by a third party, the track follows the object from the old to the new location and can extend for miles.

Once a new person thinks about the object the track is reactivated, like throwing a switch, and this connection will remain fully active for about an hour, according to Andersson, after which it slowly fades away (see chapter 6). This has exciting implications for dowsing and explains how early sea-faring peoples were able to cross oceans even on starless nights with no conventional aids to navigation.

☆ At first, locate items lost within a two-mile radius of your starting point, as it is easier to follow the psi-tracks on foot.

☆ If the missing artefact is not yours, try to hold one similar or get as vivid a description as possible and visualise it surrounded by golden light with a golden trail emanating in a straight line towards you.

☆ When you can see the track in your mind's eye, look beyond the object for any distinguishing features that will help you to identify the location.

☆ Begin to walk, using your pendulum to keep you on-course. If your pendulum is crystal you may see a radiance shining from it. You can also feel a gentle vibration under your feet. This is a common reaction when walking ley lines, ancient tracks along which travellers have endowed the land with their hopes and dreams for hundreds or even thousands of years. Ley lines are psi-tracks par excellence (see chapter 6).

☆ Your pendulum will demonstrate its travelling mode which will become stronger as you approach the object.

☆ If you feel that the trail is fading, project from your mind a beam of light just ahead of your pendulum, and in Aboriginal style weave legends or even a simple repetitive rhyme about the object.

☆ The map method is best for missing items over a long distance, and you can use the above method with a large-scale map, holding the pendulum over your present location and gently circling it clockwise while visualising the golden trail, until it responds positively, which over a map tends to be an actual clockwise circle or your 'yes' equivalent (see chapter 8).

☆ Mark down any relevant reference points *en route*, so that if you are using a bicycle or car you can stop at regular intervals and check you are still on-course by dowsing over each marker point.

☆ As your map dowsing accuracy improves you will need to stop less frequently, and in time you may identify the psi-track from the map alone.

Finding Lost Animals

At times pets may roam beyond their usual territory and become frightened or shut in an outbuilding. Earlier in the chapter I mentioned using a direction chart, but you can use the psi-track method to equally good effect.

Stroking a favourite photograph of an animal or touching the pet's bed establishes the strong psychic connection that can lead you along the route taken by the missing animal; this may be slightly convoluted.

☆ Hold the pendulum over the link and softly call your pet's name, any phrases you commonly use to call it for a meal and mentally stroke your animal and feel and smell its fur.

☆ Hear its response in your mind's ear and visualise a single piece of fur gradually expanding in your field of vision until the whole animal comes into view as though it was standing in front of you.

☆ Ask your pendulum to take you to the place where the animal will be at the time you will reach it, and ask it to give an ellipse signal just before then and to circle positively at the actual place.

☆ Ask the pendulum to give you a reverse ellipse signal if you pass it, as you practised with the direction chart.

☆ Try not to let logic intrude by calculating likely places – you will already have checked those – and in the song line tradition, retell to yourself or anyone accompanying you anecdotes about the animal, whether funny, sentimental or sad, so that you reactivate the connection, especially if you pass any of the places where you walked or played together.

☆ Keep calling the animal softly. See if the pendulum response is getting stronger. When the pendulum signals you are almost there, start calling more loudly.

☆ Once you are at the place where the pendulum indicates the animal's presence, walk in all directions, letting the strength of the pendulum's positive response determine how close you are. As I said earlier, pets will hide in the most unexpected places, so ignore logic and persist, even if there is no sign of your animal.

☆ Ask owners of sheds to search them and if necessary return the next day to call the pet's name when it may be awake.

☆ If an animal does not want to be found, you have to respect its wishes. There also the possibility that someone has adopted the animal – something which is only possible in the long term with the animal's consent in the case of a cat – and so you have to decide how long to keep watch surreptitiously.

☆ If you get no signals at all from the animal when you begin dowsing, it may have died, perhaps in a road accident, and its body may have been disposed of. Or it may have left you emotionally and become attached to someone else. Try again for two or three days, but after this grieve in your own way for your pet, perhaps lighting a candle next to its photograph, rather than endlessly searching. Leave any notices in place just in case – and in a week, a month, or even longer your pet may decide the bed was softer in its old corner and decide to come back.

Missing Persons

Only approach this area when you are very experienced, and then with great caution as it is one where many negative emotions – fear, grief, guilt – are attached. For these reasons it is very hard to find a clear positive trail. Although some missing adults are glad to be reunited with friends and family, others may have changed identity to avoid being detected.

Even if they are in destructive situations, they might not welcome intervention. At the worst you may be the bearer of bad tidings and take away any vestiges of hope for those left behind.

If children are involved, you may feel that any help is of value, although to be instrumental in locating a body rather than the live child can be heart-rending for the dowser. Sometimes such a discovery may be the only way a family can rest and grieve properly, but it is an area fraught with pain. The support of an organisation may be of immense value if you decide that you wish to use your skills in this way.

☆ If you are searching for a missing person proceed with caution, and unless you are part of an organised search party, use a map of the area for your initial exploration. Locate where you feel the person is – your pendulum may transmit strong emotions as well as directions. Offer this information to police or a missing persons bureau rather than approaching the family. Increasingly, police are taking dowsing seriously.

☆ First you need to establish a link with the missing person. A photograph or possession can be invaluable, even a photo from a newspaper, or if you can make contact with someone who knew the subject well, you may be able to establish a link via the third person's affections.

☆ Try and find out from newspaper reports the exact clothes the person was wearing when he or she was last seen, and if possible visit the location of the last verified sighting. This will give you the spot from which to begin your search initially on a map and later by walking out the route using your pendulum.

Because it is not possible to approach this area free from emotion, the problem is the reverse from that of dowsing for inanimate objects so any practice may be helpful.

☆ If you would like to develop your ability to locate missing persons, you will need to practise with a familiar subject, perhaps one of the family or a close friend.

☆ Wait until he or she is travelling even a few miles away where there are a variety of potential locations and no clear pattern; ask only what he or she will be wearing. Pre-arrange times for him or her to pause and make detailed notes of their location and actions so that you can compare them with yours later.

☆ At half-hourly intervals for a period of three or four hours, draw a sketch map of say different shops in a shopping mall with which you and the subject are familiar, or of an area of the country, and let your pendulum indicate when you are on target. Note the time, location and as many details as come to you, for example that the subject was talking to a man in a hat who stopped to ask for directions.

☆ If this sounds remarkably like clairvoyance or remote viewing (see my book: *Psychic Awareness: A Piatkus Guide* (Piatkus, 1999)) that is because these powers are involved in dowsing. There are no clear demarcations between psychic abilities, and the pendulum is a tangible way of expressing and confirming them in the external world.

Archaeological Dowsing

Another area where dowsers can practise their skills openly is archaeological dowsing. A master of this craft is Brian Slade, President of the Sheppey Archaeological Society, an archaeologist, astronomer, historian, author and broadcaster with more than 20 published books on archaeology, history and associated subjects to his name. The history of the Isle of Sheppey, which lies off the Kent coast in south-east England, goes back to the Bronze Age and Brian has worked tirelessly to uncover buried archaeological treasures. He has the uncanny and yet quite natural ability to dowse with unerring accuracy the location of buried treausre that holds the key to the area's rich history.

In the early days, like other dowser-archaeologists who wanted their ability to be kept secret so that their discoveries would be taken seriously, Brian invented an ancient map of the projected complete Norman Minster and Anglo-Saxon Monasterium Sexburgha complex (the Abbey of St Sexburgha) at Minster on the Isle of Sheppey, to explain away his uncannily accurate findings to officials and expert bodies.

However, when Brian was very ill in hospital he realised that it was important to acknowledge openly this ability. He told me: 'I began dowsing back in the 1960s with the GEC (General Electricity Company) when looking for cables on old sites. The problem was that 60 or 70 years ago when the cables were first put down, the location of earthing strips would be marked on plans. But once the engineer had left the site, the navvies would, to save time, place the cables via the most direct route and sell any spare copper to a scrap merchant. Therefore many of these early plans were useless. It was not possible to use metal detectors on site where there were many cables and so much magnetism.'

So Brian resorted to earth magic to find the cables and it worked. 'Now I use my dowsing gift to uncover historical remains. I still use my bent welding rods or hazel twigs.'

In 1993, Brian carried out his detailed dowsing survey of Minster on the Isle of Sheppey. It convinced him that much of the hilltop where he lived overlaid the remains of a 7th- to 9th-century Anglo-Saxon nunnery, an 11th- to 16th-century Norman Abbey and a cemetery. Brian and his local team have uncovered the remains precisely where he predicted they would be. 'Time and time again,' he says, 'it has been shown that if the digging had been even a yard on either side of the spot indicated by the dowsing, nothing of significance would have been found. For example, I asked a lady living in Minster village if I might dig up part of her back garden lawn. She agreed with some trepidation and we promptly unearthed seven 7th- and 9th-century Anglo-Saxon bronze dress pins, post hole evidence of 7th- to 9th-century timber buildings, an Anglo-Saxon coin dating back to AD 737 – AD 758, four Henry II long cross silver pennies, examples of Anglo-Saxon glass, ten varieties of Roman pottery and as much Anglo-Saxon Ipswich-type pottery as produced by all the excavations at Canterbury combined. It was a veritable treasure trove.

'At last, thanks to such finds, my booklets and vigorous campaigning, several areas of Minster on Sheppey have become scheduled areas of major archaeological importance which means that no-one can dig up the area or build on it without permission.'

EXERCISE: SEEKING ANTIQUES

I would not advise that you start excavations on a recognised site of antiquity as you may encounter all kinds of legal problems as well as perhaps unwittingly damaging precious clues to the past. However, you can often enrol on day or weekend courses involving archaeological digs or fossil hunting, and if you are subtle you can ask your pendulum to indicate when it is directly over something of historical value.

Best of all, visit a museum that has artefacts of all ages and start by visiting the museum shop.

☆ Buy either a brochure, a few replica coins, a piece of pottery or a small piece of jewellery copied from an artefact of several thousand years ago. If you have bought an object, ascertain that the original is in the museum itself.

☆ Select a photograph from the brochure of an ancient artefact, study every detail and read what you can about it.

☆ Alternatively, choose one of the coins or the piece of jewellery and hold it with your eyes closed, letting your fingers absorb the vibes you get even in a replica. This is the psychic art of psychometry, another ability that will be useful to you (see my book: *Psychic Awareness: A Piatkus Guide* (Piatkus, 1999)).

☆ Hold your pendulum over the object or picture and ask your pendulum to take you by the most direct accessible route to the case in which the artefact is kept.

☆ If you visit a museum early or late in the day it will not be crowded, but hold your pendulum, especially if it is a pendant, close to your body so that it will not attract attention. If the museum is really crowded, hold the pendulum, perhaps concealed by a scarf or coat, and ask it to direct you by tugging or vibrating.

☆ Avoid following any direction signs – trust your pendulum. Sometimes the route recommended by the museum curator is not the most direct, but the best for the flow of human traffic.

☆ Let your pendulum lead you to the case or exhibit. Stand to the left of the case and ask the pendulum to continue to move until it is directly in front of the artefact.

☆ Once you are practised, you can go to areas near the sea and marshes, as well as those of known antiquity, where the land has recently been disturbed by erosion or building work and allow your pendulum to guide you to places to dig. The field next to an ancient monument or ruined castle will contain stones that share the ancient vibrations of the place, and if you hold them they will reveal images, feelings and even sounds of the past that, though less tangible than a Roman coin or Bronze Age pin, may nevertheless link you with earlier ages.

5

Dowsing
and
Health

Pendulums operate as aerials or transmitters of psychic energy, and as such they can channel positive healing forces into our bodies from the natural world, from the sun and moon, from trees and flowers. They can also amplify and transmit out innate healing energies into those who need them. The crystal pendulum with its living energies is especially powerful as a healing tool because of its association with the forces of Earth, Air, Fire and Water. The ancient Greeks believed these forces to be the elements which make up all life, and they are still recognised as symbols of spiritual strength and wholeness.

My own first spontaneous experience of healing dowsing energies came when I first acquired an L-shaped metal dowsing rod and was trying it out on a beach near my home on the Isle of Wight. I have gall bladder problems that resurface when I eat irregularly, and because of a long television session with the BBC in Southampton I had missed breakfast and lunch. The children were eager that I took them out before tea and my gall bladder was beginning to make its dissatisfaction with these arrangements very apparent. To take my mind off my discomfort while the children played in the sea, I planned to hunt for coins or fossils using the rod, and walked along the sand waiting for some sign of treasure from the dowsing rod.

Suddenly it swung violently to the north-west and I felt a surge of relief as though a warm charge was running down my arm through my body. I looked up and saw the brilliant full moon rising over the cliffs on a warm summer evening. The feeling of relief continued until I turned away to watch the children to make sure they were not swimming out too far. The pain returned.

When I had checked the children, I let the dowsing rod guide me back on to the 'moon path' and the relief continued. The effect was magnified when I took my crystal pendulum out of my bag and held the crystal instead of the rod, so that the moon was reflected in it. This transmitted the warmth and radiance one would feel from a heat lamp through my body, although I was not holding the pendulum directly over my stomach.

Subsequent tests have convinced me that the waxing moon will transmit gentle energies through a rod or pendulum while the waning moon soothes and calms. The fact that I had not looked for the moon suggests that my response on the beach was not due to a placebo effect.

Healing with Nature

According to the Chinese philosophy of feng shui and the Western theories of geomancy, currents of energy are all around us, some negative and some positive. By tuning into positive forces emanating from trees, flowers or flowing surface water using your pendulum, you can receive *prana* or the life force that is present in all living matter, in an amplified form.

☆ If you are feeling tired or stressed, find a green open space, preferably deep country near a stream. Your garden, a town square or even the smallest of public parks will offer the focus you need if you have only a short time or limited resources.

☆ Concentrate upon your current physical needs: extra energy, peace of mind or relief from pain.

☆ Begin by slowly turning in a circle, holding your pendulum until you feel a positive current surging up from a natural focus with which you have established a resonance, such as a tree, a pond or a pile of rocks. This force may be experienced as a tingling sensation or warm liquid running through the divining tool into your arm, and from there to the part of the body which needs a boost from nature or throughout your whole form.

Healing Others with the Life Force

As well as helping to fill yourself with new life and energy, the pendulum can divert energy from nature via the diviner to another person who needs healing. If you work with family members or close friends, the love between you will strengthen the natural healing energies.

☆ If your pendulum is used for other purposes, such as divination or dowsing for lost objects, it should be cleansed before healing work by holding it under running water. It will need recharging frequently. Alternatively, you could keep a special crystal pendulum for healing work, either the traditional clear quartz or amethyst or rose quartz, which are natural healing stones.

☆ When healing using natural forces, focus the pendulum on a specific area of pain or discomfort.

☆ Alternatively, hold the pendulum above the head of the sick or distressed person and let the healing powers enter his or her aura via the Crown chakra, a psychic energy centre in the middle of the crown of the head. This aura can, with practice, be detected either externally or in the mind's eye, especially around the head; it is frequently depicted around the heads of saints in medieval art as a halo. For more information on auras see my book. *The Complete Guide to Psychic Development* (Piatkus, 1997).

☆ You do not need to be able to *see* the aura to heal it. As with all psychic work, begin by visualising a golden halo of rainbow coloured circles emanating from the head. These are most easily 'seen' in a mirror lit by candle light or lamps. In time you will no longer need to visualise.

☆ Before you begin healing work, invoke protection. Directing healing energies can be a very exhausting process.

☆ Focus on a rich green plant or brightly coloured flowers: a poinsettia in winter, daffodils in spring, roses in summer and golden chrysanthemums in autumn. Alternatively, use seasonal flowers that are indigenous in your own region, or if you prefer, focus on golden fruit that is bursting with the life force: oranges, melons, pineapples.

☆ Hold your pendulum initially at eye level so that you can see light reflected through the crystal and can feel the strong tingling of the life force flowing through you like a laser beam of gold and then on to the subject.

☆ If you can, work in a pool of sunlight or full moonlight. A gold or silver candle to represent solar and lunar rays can be substituted after dusk and during a dark day.

☆ Begin breathing rhythmically, absorbing the golden light emanating from the flower or fruit via the pendulum and flowing through you to establish a circuit. You may feel warm, especially in the hand holding the pendulum.

☆ When both you and the pendulum are filled with healing light, place the pendulum about 5cm (2in) from the afflicted area, over the head of the subject, or in the direction of the person you are healing if he or she is absent.

☆ Close your eyes and feel or see in your mind's eye the energy pulsating in ever-increasing clockwise circles out through the divining tool towards its target.

☆ Your pendulum should begin to turn clockwise at this point. If it does not, make two or three initial circles and wait for it to take over. Continue for two or three minutes.

☆ Remember to close down your own energies after healing so that they are not buzzing around in your head all day, preventing you sleeping at night. The star technique which you met when trying to empty your mind for dowsing has many uses in psychic work and is one to which most people can relate.

☆ When you have finished, recharge your pendulum as described in chapter 2. Thank your guardians and try to relax for a few hours or spend time in the open air on purely physical work.

Identifying Energy Pathways and Removing Blockages

It may be that there is no direct correlation between the site of a pain and its source. Many people, especially from Eastern cultures, believe that our bodies are criss-crossed by a network of energy pathways. A system from India identifies spheres within the body called chakras as whirling coloured energies, each of which relate to a bodily area and function. Oriental medicine calls the energy lines which join different organs of the body 'meridians'.

But you do not need to explore any of these philosophies, or even subscribe to the concept of specific psychic energy paths, to accept the idea that our body, mind and soul are interlinked and that a blockage or disorder in one area will affect the whole system.

Given practice, almost anyone can tune into their bodily energy ebbs and flows using a pendulum, and this is a very effective way not only of monitoring your health and energy levels, but also of restoring any imbalance and clearing any blockages. The normal positive movement of the pendulum will help to indicate the pathways of energy through your own body or that of another person if you hold the pendulum about 5cm (2in) above the body.

☆ Begin by tracing a path from the feet upwards, clearing your mind of preconceptions and allowing the pendulum to guide you on your unique formation of inner leys that may vary according to the season, the time of day and external pressures that stimulate or depress your internal ebbs and flows.

☆ When your pendulum encounters a blockage it will either stop or swing in the reverse direction and feel heavy.

☆ You can give healing by first drawing out pain by consciously circling the pendulum anti-clockwise nine times over the blockage and visualising either a tangled knot melting or darkness flowing out.

☆ Before using your pendulum for energising the body, hold it up to the sunlight or to full moonlight, to a source of *prana* or life force, or plunge it into a glass of spring water to cleanse it, shaking it dry. I have only recently added this stage to healing work, but find that it does help to ensure that a clear flow of light enters the body.

☆ Pass the energised pendulum nine times clockwise over the now cleared blockage to revitalise the area. You may detect a faint golden glow around the area or person and the pendulum and your pendulum hand may feel quite hot.

Dowsing for Remedies

A pendulum should never be used as a substitute for medical advice from a qualified practitioner. If a pain or symptom persists or becomes acute, it does not mean that you have failed. Your pendulum healing may take time and can work happily alongside conventional physicians or homeopathic remedies over a period of weeks or even months.

If a variety of alternative over-the-counter conventional or herbal remedies, vitamin or mineral supplements are on offer for a particular condition from which you are suffering, dowse for the one that will be most helpful to you in your present state of health. If you do need to visit a physician or homeopath, there are normally a variety of treatments for the same illness, and unless there are contra-indications such as high blood pressure that may make one method unsafe, you can ask to go away and decide on the treatment you will follow, dowsing over the names of the drugs or therapies until your pendulum indicates the most suitable. There are also many ways of taking a herb or substance – as an infusion, in tablets, a tincture, a massage or even added to bath water. You can discover the most effective form by dowsing over the alternatives as I have suggested or use a question and answer method. Either is as effective for this and the questioning format can also be applied to any health matter where the choice is slightly more complex.

Questions and Answers

☆ Begin by asking your pendulum whether taking a remedy in the immediate future (as opposed to the moment of purchasing) will be helpful.

☆ If the answer is negative, ask pertinent questions, for example whether you need to modify your diet before taking the medicine, to rest, or allow nature to take its course before embarking on an invasive course of treatment.

☆ If the results run counter to medical advice, go back and speak to the physician or pharmacist as there may be factors he or she had not appreciated at the time of prescription.

☆ If we can listen to our own bodies and inner voices to make informed choices, we can use medication to its best advantage. Often the pendulum will raise deep-seated doubts that need resolution and occasionally conventional pharmaceutical products can have quite dramatic side effects.

☆ If you have a number of herbal remedies at home or have a friendly health store, you can hold your pendulum over each relevant bottle or packet, asking to be shown a positive response or a 'This One' tugging movement over the most appropriate remedy for your current condition.

☆ Alternatively, create a grid chart, divide it into as many options as you need, write a name or herb in each, or if this is not a natural number for division, draw one or two extra segments and leave them blank. You may wish to add brief descriptions of each, plus any doubts or plus points.

☆ Hold your pendulum over each of the labelled segments in turn, and if necessary go over the grid a second time.

☆ If two segments have the same positive response you can perhaps combine them as this can be very effective with herbal remedies, but always check with a herbalist or pharmacist first.

Flower Remedies

Flower and tree essences are an area in which dowsing may be involved, not only in the choice of remedies, but in the original creation of some varieties.

Flower essences are extracted from wild flowers and sometimes tree blossoms that work on negative emotional states, transforming them into a more positive response. The healing properties of flower essences are linked with the life force of flowers, each flower's unique energies corresponding with a human emotion. They are said to be a more concentrated form of *pranic* light, because, as the name implies, they contain the essence of the species.

The healing power of flowers was well known to the Ancient Egyptians and Australian Aborigines, however, flower essences were first created by Dr Edward Bach during the 1930s in England. From these original 38 remedies have evolved thousands of flower essences being produced around the world using native flowers and trees.

Bailey Flower Essences: Dr Arthur Bailey first discovered the Bach Flower Essences when he had a post-viral illness and the wife of his homeopathic doctor used dowsing to identify the correct remedies for his condition. After his successful treatment, Dr Bailey himself began dowsing around his garden to discover flowers with healing properties, often in answer to a patient's specific need. Over 11 years he came up with about 20 new remedies by this method. He became convinced that the majority of illnesses stemmed from the mind and its attitude to the world, so that until a person can live at peace with themselves and the world, the body will continue to reflect the resulting conflicts (see Useful Addresses for further information on flower remedies).

Dowsing for a Flower Remedy: With hundreds of flower remedies to choose from, it can be difficult to find the right one or the right combination. For example, sufferers from depression are faced with a bewildering array of choices, even from the Bach range. To select the most appropriate remedies, read all accompanying literature and set aside those recommended for alleviating depression. Place these in a clockwise circle so that each bottle touches, with the labels facing away from you, and move the pendulum over each remedy. The pendulum will give a strong positive response over certain bottles and circle negatively over the others.

Food and Dowsing

You can extend this category to all oral input – food, drink, alcohol and cigarettes – so that the pendulum can help not only with allergies (see chapter 2 for an example of divining food allergies), but with any compulsions or addictions that may mask deeper needs through a desire for instant oral satisfaction.

☆ Through careful and honest questioning each time you feel out of control, the pendulum may reveal why you *crave* as opposed to *need* a particular substance. Would it be possible to wait a while or substitute an alternative less addictive or health-threatening product, activity or treat that would bring equal pleasure?

☆ Could you limit the amount of the potentially harmful substance taken and gradually reduce it, using your pendulum and a timing circle?

☆ When you feel an overwhelming desire to binge on junk food or light up one too many cigarettes, pause and question your true feelings and needs with your pendulum and you may find that the time lapse, the calm induced by writing down questions or options and passing your pendulum over them, and the attention to *yourself*, actually reduce the blind urgency and sense of panic.

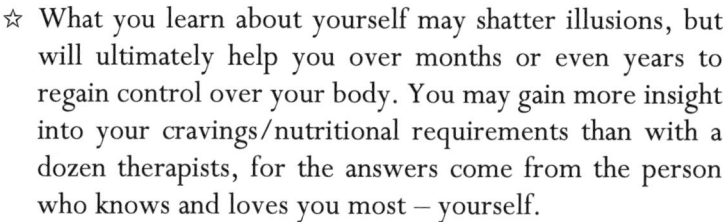

☆ What you learn about yourself may shatter illusions, but will ultimately help you over months or even years to regain control over your body. You may gain more insight into your cravings/nutritional requirements than with a dozen therapists, for the answers come from the person who knows and loves you most – yourself.

EXERCISE: SENDING LOVE AND LIGHT THROUGH THE PENDULUM

The pendulum is a powerful amplifier for sending love and light not only to those who are sick or unhappy, but to absent family members or close friends or to someone from whom you are estranged.

☆ Find a quiet place and time and light a candle: *white* for creative energy and healing, *green* for love and lovers, *red* for anyone under threat, *pink* for reconciliation and for friendship, children and animals, *orange* for people setting out on a new separate path or searching for a new role, *purple* for spirituality, *blue* for people concerned about their career and for travellers, *yellow* for anyone who is studying or needs to be logical and *brown* for older people.

☆ Place the candle behind the pendulum. Spin your pendulum gently so that the candle light reflects through it, and as you look at the spiralling light, project into the pendulum, as if looking through a window, an image of the person of whom you are thinking.

☆ Speak either aloud or in your mind the words you would like the absent or estranged person to hear and visualise him or her smiling in response and perhaps holding out a hand.

☆ Turn the pendulum even faster so that the colour blurs.

☆ When your pendulum spontaneously reverses direction, blow out the candle, sending the love and light to the face in the crystal.

☆ If possible, follow this with a small token of love if relations are cordial with the absent person.

☆ If there is coldness, make some form of non-confrontational contact, perhaps a friendly card or a brief meeting at a place you know the person to visit. Even if reconciliation does not follow, you have the knowledge that you have started to heal your own wound.

☆ If you feel negatively towards someone who has wronged you, send him or her love and light through the pendulum. Bad thoughts only multiply and clog up the universe. Who knows? You may get a nice letter or phone call in return.

6

Earth Energies

Earth energies are natural powers that we can feel not only at sacred sites where yang and yin, male and female energies unite, but also pulsating beneath our feet on open land or in the smallest garden and through our fingertips when we hold a crystal or stone or touch a tree or flower. They can be manifest as earth lights that hover over plains or rocks, or as strange animals such as the legendary demon Black Dog of East Anglia.

A pendulum, especially one made of crystal, will respond to these energies in a way that virtually no other instrument can, transmitting their positive healing and energising powers spontaneously and warning if the earth energies are over-whelming or potentially negative in a home or workplace through which leys or underground streams run.

The Magic of Stones

To experience the full magnificence of earth energies, visit one of the ancient stone circles that may date from as early as

3500 BC, such as Newgrange in County Meath in Ireland, perhaps the most spectacular prehistoric cemetery in the world and close to the sacred hill of Tara, seat of the ancient Irish High Kings. Other centres of natural power include the stone ships circle in Vastmanland in Sweden, the stone circle at Almendras in Portugal which may have been created as a temple to the stars, Stonehenge on Salisbury Plain, or the stone Medicine Wheels of North America, such as the Big Horn Medicine Wheel near Sheridan in Wyoming.

My own favourite stone circles are at Avebury in Wiltshire which, unlike many ancient monuments in Britain, are still accessible to the public (see my book: *Ghost Encounters*, (Blandford, 1999) for more details of ley lines and sacred sites).

Power Centres

Whether you visit one of the many great monuments or a single standing stone near to your home, the principle is the same. Where there are sacred rock paintings or natural rock sculptures that have become a focus for ritual or an ancient chalk figure, you can experience spiralling power through your pendulum.

These power centres are believed by some geomancers and dowsers to be places where natural cosmic energy enters the earth at a point where there are underground water domes – where water rises vertically from deep in the earth. Cosmic energy, which forms ley lines at these points, is regarded in almost every culture as yang, positive and masculine, emanating from the sky, the power of the Sky Father. Water is yin, negative in the electrical sense and female, flowing from the womb of the Earth Mother. At sites where these energies met and harmonised, such was the experience of spiritual and physical power and well-being that they were chosen as places of worship thousands of years ago. Others say that these sites are where an intersection of underground streams are crossed by an energy ley, perhaps even two. The feelings are the same.

Linking Into the Energies at a Power Centre

Walk around the site with your pendulum, asking it to locate the epicentre of power. Your pendulum will perhaps spin powerfully first in one direction and then the other, continuing to spiral. You may also feel as if your whole body is glowing and pulsating. Your pendulum will become charged with power which you may see as a light within the crystal.

To me, dowsing at ancient sites seems intended to uplift the soul and connect us with the timelessness of the universe, rather than measuring the size of a dome or the exit points of the veins of water or assessing the source and nature of the perceived energies as a way of verifying the experience. For this reason, although you may wish to assess your findings when you have worked on physical dowsing, even as a total novice you can tune into these energies – you would find it difficult not to.

Whatever your focus, the best teachers of earth energy dowsing are lovers of the countryside, be they a Native American or city dweller, who instinctively feels the movement of each blade of grass and the pain of a dying flower.

☆ Go to places where earth lights, corn circles or alien encounters have been reported – one theory links ley lines and power centres with markers and landing sites for UFOs, rather like giant airport runways.

☆ Choose a transition time – New Year's Eve, Hallowe'en which is the Celtic New Year or May Eve, the start of the

Celtic summer – and you will find that the energies are especially powerful and easy to access.

☆ Study a plan or picture of a circle or site as it was originally, so that you can see the form when it was first used for worship and ceremony.

☆ There may be stones missing, but if you allow your feet and pendulum to guide you, you will find that your course around the old circles is similar to a Maypole dance.

☆ As you follow the spiralling energies reflected in your spinning pendulum, you will 'see' the circle as it was. It is no accident that Maypole dances involve tangling ribbons around a central axis representing the world tree that was believed in northern mythology to support the realms of heaven, earth and underworld.

☆ Dance with your pendulum (it not only liberates your mind and body but can also be an excellent way of getting rid of your family if you wish to dowse alone!).

☆ Ley energies are sometimes located at ancient monuments, not only at the epicentre, but in straight lines along ancient avenues of stones leading from the circles, and in some cases following these can help you to identify the true centre. At sites such as Avebury and Stonehenge they form the hub of a wheel of intersecting leys.

☆ If you hold your energised pendulum over a part of your body where you feel discomfort, or run it over your entire frame from about 5cm (2in) away, you should experience relief from pain and tension and assume a sense of well-being and spiritual enlightenment. It is said that even experienced dowsers get different reactions at sacred sites because our interaction with earth forces is unique.

If you are having difficulty following the leys from the centre, try the West Kennet Avenue at Avebury: two rows of parallel stones that run from the circles at Avebury a mile and a half to a smaller circle of stone and wood posts called the Sanctuary above East Kennet village. On the Avenue you can still see the diamond female and pointed male stones that were the focus of fertility magic. Originally, there was also another parallel avenue. Some dowsers argue that West Kennet was a deliberately constructed alignment for ceremonial purposes and not built on a true energy ley, but I have felt the energies very strongly there. These powers may be the accumulated hopes, fears and prayers of those who over the centuries built up a ley line – we cannot always isolate a source. I am convinced that ley lines do increase or decrease over the centuries and are interactive rather than fixed forces.

A sacred place such as Carnac in Brittany has many avenues still standing, and the pull of the earth is immense – the pendulum becomes almost red-hot in Brittany as it spirals around the many ancient stones and sites in this region. Indeed, Brittany has more megaliths than anywhere in the world.

Anywhere on or close to these sites, not only at the power centre, the reaction of your pendulum may be quite unlike its normal dowsing response, but if you ask it to guide you only on paths of healing, you will experience a close connection with the natural world and with the past.

☆ You may see or sense shadowy guardians of the place or those who danced and sang over the millennia.

☆ You may experience warm as opposed to cold spots where the energies are strong.

☆ Note any special dreams you have on the night after you have visited the site. If possible, try to stay in the area, in a homely rather than modern hotel.

☆ If you can visit the stones at sunrise or sunset with your pendulum, especially on a day when that particular stone circle is aligned to the mid-winter or summer solstice as many are, you will gain more psychic impressions than from a whole library of psychic books. The Internet offers sites that will provide such information and plans of the original form, but a good guide book will serve the same purpose.

☆ Place your pendulum on a stone at sunrise and it will be filled with healing power.

Ley Energies

There is often a distinction made between energy leys and true ley lines, although the definition of the latter does contain many variations. Energy leys are said to be 2–3m (6–8ft) wide beams of yang energy and these energy leys do often coincide with alignments of ancient sacred buildings along them, precisely because our ancestors were drawn instinctively to these places of spiritual power.

True ley lines, the ancient straight traders' tracks first identified by Alfred Watkins in the 1920s, are the most stringently defined, having at least five aligned pre-Reformation sacred sites within a relatively short distance, say ten miles, that can be measured as straight to the standard of an H pencil line on a 1:25,000 scale map.

Post-reformation structures were no longer necessarily built on energy leys because the instinctive awareness of the powers diminished. The Benedictines in the Middle Ages had great knowledge of these spiritual energies, and wherever you find one of their abbeys you will discover a ley running through. But such strict definitions may actually exclude many existing ley lines, for example in the US where Native American sacred sites may have been destroyed and where many sacred edifices are post-Reformation, but again may have been instinctively created on a site of spiritual power by the early colonists. In lands of greater dimensions than England, sacred sites may be hundreds of miles apart.

Some energy leys, even in the UK, are not marked by places of power at all. You can detect these quite spontaneously as you walk across vast open tracts of land; you may see natural markers, a huge rock on top of a hill, clumps of hawthorns that were tended by secret village guardians to guide travellers, or ponds. These areas are not built on except by Mother Nature. If you begin in an open hilly region at a rocky outcrop, your pendulum will respond with a positive circling movement along the way and you will feel the energy vibrating beneath your feet.

Solar and Lunar Energies and the Earth

Fractures or changes in the earth's crust can be caused by the pull of gravity from the sun and moon. The interplay of these two vast energy forces vary over the moon's monthly cycle, and the annual passage of the earth around the sun causes twisting, stretching and cracking of the earth's crust in such a way that the resulting faults and released water may change the nature and intensity of earth energies, thus affecting humans, plants, insects and animals. Dowse for these effects, which may be beneficial or harmful, at times of the full moon or at noon, the height of the sun's power, in your home and place of work, especially if you feel that certain areas are always dark even in bright sunlight or warm and light even in winter. Or you may find that quarrels break out at this point or people complain of tension headaches or a stiff neck when sitting in that area.

If your pendulum makes a positive response over a particular area it may be a good room in which to grow plants, sleep or relax. However, if there is a negative response you can neutralise the effects using the methods suggested later in this chapter. Animals tend to be attracted to these spots if the energy is beneficial, so dowse over your cat's favourite corner and perhaps take it over for your own leisure activities.

Negative Earth Energies

Though our ancestors built their temples and abbeys on ley lines, few people built houses on them because the power was so overwhelming, especially where leys crossed. In Ireland today few would erect a building on what is known as a fairy path, which stretches between ancient hill forts. What is more, the natural flow of earth energies may have become blocked by such building work. Major construction works such as motorways or existing or former mine workings can also sour the energy. It is said that not only are people, animals and plants adversely affected, but even telegraph poles seem to corrode faster over these spots of negative energy.

Some researchers attribute negative forces to Hartmann and Curry energy fields. These are named after their discoverers and are said to divide the earth into square lattices, that in the case of a Curry lattice is about 4m square and the lines themselves about 40cm wide. The Hartmann lines are said to run almost as the geographical longitudinal and latitudinal lines, only deviating by ten degrees and are about 20cm wide and 1.5m apart. Where two Curry lines or two Hartmann lines cross, strong energies occur; where a Curry and a Hartmann line cross the effect is doubled.

But some expert dowsers such as Dr Arthur Bailey who created the Bailey Flower Remedies (see chapter 5) believe that the influence of geopathic stress can be felt about 3m on either side of a ley line or underground stream. Sin Lonegren, former head of the Dowsing School of the American Society of Dowsers, also says that energy leys are 2 to 3m wide.

Trouble can be expected, as with the Curry/Hartmann concept, especially where these energies cross. But Dr Bailey points out that, except in old mine shafts, water will not run along a straight course and so a grid theory would not account for black streams.

Black Streams

Although some people refer to all negative earth energies as black streams, others restrict the term to those of the vast network of underground veins of water that have become soured or polluted psychically, and sometimes physically, for those reasons I have listed above. Dwellings or workplaces built on black streams may seem dark and damp even on a summer's day, and may seem to create a hostile working environment in which there are frequent absences for minor and sometimes stress-related illnesses.

Because there are so many theories concerning the nature and extent of these negative energies and how to neutralise them, I have presented the major concepts and would suggest that as you dowse you see which accords most with your own findings.

Neutralising Negative Earth Energies

Although we may not fully understand earth energies, there are a variety of methods you can use to neutralise any areas of negativity detected by your pendulum at earth or home. What I do find intriguing is that if you apply the remedy for the theory to which you subscribe, it works! Wishful thinking? No, because people who enter a house or workplace from which negative earth energies have gone, comment on the improved atmosphere and imagine that it has been redecorated. Family members or work colleagues who know nothing of the dowsing work also spontaneously find an improvement in health and a reduction in stress levels within a few weeks or even days.

☆ Try dowsing with your pendulum around the workplace or home and see where your pendulum makes powerful negative circles and fills you with a sense of foreboding or even makes you shiver. This damp coldness is very different from the crisp cold air that is sensed around ghosts as two dimensions meet.

☆ At each point when you are dowsing around the environment, ask your pendulum to: 'Show me by your negative response if there are negative earth energies here that may be detrimental to health and well-being.'

☆ Plot each place where you experience the negative swing of the pendulum on a chart of your home or workplace (see chapter 8). You may find a wavy line which would indicate water, or a straight line for a ley, or even a grid pattern in which case the pendulum may spin round negatively several times.

☆ Continue to go around your home or workplace with your pendulum until you have identified all the negative spots.

☆ Ask your pendulum if you have now located all the negative earth energies in the immediate area. If it says 'No', use either a map dowsing technique or your direction chart and dowse as though looking for a lost object (see chapter 4).

☆ Use your pendulum to assess how wide a spot is by asking it to cease swinging when it has reached the outer limits.

☆ If you find a Curry and Hartmann cross, that may be indicated by the pendulum continuing to spiral in a negative direction. Neutralise the effect outdoors by placing a rock on top of the cross; indoors, the movement of a chair, bed or desk to a more congenial spot in the room may give instant improvement.

☆ Even if you follow the underground water/ley concepts which hypothesise much wider bands of energy, you can still escape from the centre of the source and the most powerful energies by moving a bed about half a metre, supplementing the neutralisation by methods described later in this chapter.

☆ The first step with any negative energies in a room at home or at work is to move any furniture as far from the centre of the spot as possible, or to change your room arrangement so that you rest and work in congenial spots. Phone calls and personal interviews at work should be carried out from a place of positive energies; storage areas are less important.

☆ If you cannot make major rearrangements at work, ensure that you always have fresh flowers or a pot plant above the spot of negative power to absorb any bad feelings. You may need to replace these frequently as it is not a conducive spot for growth, so try to rotate plants.

☆ Amethyst crystals are perhaps the most effective stones for neutralising all forms of negative earth energies. Small amethyst inclusions, still in the rock, are not expensive and make excellent paperweights or ornaments. Rose quartz will also take away any jagged edges of harsh energy. Position these near the centre of the spot of negative energy.

☆ Charge the amethyst as you did your pendulum before use and wash and recharge it every week or when it becomes dull.

☆ Another method is to take your pendulum outside your home and ask it to indicate the negative entry point of any black stream or negative ley. Just above this, hammer either an iron or copper rod or long nail into the ground so that no-one will hurt themselves by tripping on it. These are traditional methods of protection and those generally favoured by experts in geopathic stress.

☆ Ask the pendulum which is the right metal, either using an options chart or circle or by asking about each in turn.

☆ Using the number chart from chapter 3, ask your pendulum to indicate how many rods you need, how many centimetres thick and how close they should be to neutralise this particular negative energy flow.

☆ Another device I have seen in Hampshire is a 'dobby' stone blocking the point of negative entry. An ancient East Anglian and northern European charm for controlling the winds, this is a stone with either a natural or a carved indentation in the top into which was traditionally placed milk and honey. You can improvise with a natural stone flower container, and you may prefer to insert a small amethyst or fresh seasonal flowers to get the positive life force flowing.

☆ If you have a guardian angel with whom you make contact, ask him or her to enclose the house with love and light. Lighting pure white candles at the four compass points of a room will also dispel darker energies.

☆ Now, as you walk around the same spots, ask your pendulum to identify any remaining noxious energy. This will be indicated by a negative swing, and should be countered by burning a cleansing incense such as pine or cedar regularly over these spots until they are clear. ·

Exercise: Dowsing with your plants

Like humans, plants are believed to have an aura around them. Kirlian photography, a method which captures aura images, has shown that when part of a plant is cut off the aura of the missing part remains. Experiments involving attaching electrodes to plants have revealed that they do respond positively not only to kind words but also to thought forms, and can become distressed if someone not only hurts, but plans to harm another plant close by. In chapter 5 you took healing energies from a plant; now you are going to strengthen your plant using positive earth energies. This can be especially helpful if a plant acts as a shield for negative earth energies in your office.

☆ Hold your pendulum about 2.5cm (1in) from your favourite plant.

☆ Ask your pendulum to respond positively only when it encounters the plant aura.

☆ Slowly pass the pendulum clockwise around the outline of the plant and it should swing positively and gently as it encounters the aura.

☆ Gradually move the pendulum further away and keep passing it round the plant until you have reached the outer limits of the aura and the pendulum makes only a neutral response.

☆ Now move the pendulum slowly in and out of the aura space, asking to be shown any tears or weakness in the aura by a negative response. These would be revealed by the pendulum long before any browning or withering of leaves.

☆ There may not be any problems, but it is always beneficial to add positive energies even to a totally healthy plant.

☆ Find a place outdoors where there are positive earth energies, which may be a spot where birds settle and where there is already luxuriant growth of grass or greenery. If indoors, plants thrive in such a corner, which always seems warm, even if it is out of the sun or a winter's day, and you also may instinctively sit there.

☆ Hold your pendulum over the spot and ask your pendulum to confirm whether it has positive earth energies.

☆ If so, slowly circle your pendulum nine times (it may do this spontaneously) and visualise pure crystalline water rising in a spout and swirling around the pendulum, seeing healing waters from the Earth Mother being drawn up.

☆ Imagine next the yang energy of the leys streaming upwards as golden light. In these visualisations you are absorbing the essence of these powers.

☆ When your pendulum feels light and vibrant, it may start spiralling in a positive direction. Spin it above your plants and let the healing essence cascade down on to every leaf. This will heal any holes or darkness in the aura and in the healthy plant will promote growth. Do this weekly and you will see your plant become green, tall and strong.

☆ When you sit in your positive earth place in either house or garden, carry out the same process with your pendulum, showering on yourself the healing essence.

7

Pendulums
and Ghosts

This chapter stands at a crossroads in pendulum exploration. In chapter 6, I talked about using a pendulum to tune into ley lines and earth energies; tales of ghost sightings, legendary beings and mysterious events abound along and close to these psychic energy lines.

The pendulum is remarkably sensitive at picking up these presences and pinpointing places where leys cross or psychic energies are especially strong. At these key spots particularly, dramatic persona or semi-mythical events are usually described in local legends. If you subsequently explore the history and folk tales of ley places, you will usually find a white lady, a malevolent monk or a wild black dog who terrifies travellers, being reported not once but many times over a period of years. These ghost stories often embroidered over time are nevertheless usually based on some strange occurrence whose actual date may be lost in the mists of time. On the Isle of Wight where I live, I have continued to explore the connection between leys, legends and pendulum response. The concept seems to hold true in any area where you find old tales of mystery.

In chapter 4, I described Andersson's theory of psi-tracks, akin to the Aboriginal song lines, which would explain why a single character appears in a variety of places and guises, perhaps marking the trail trodden by ancient travellers across the island to the sea. Did these travellers wandering along the misty leys and spying a huge rock or standing stone looming ahead tell tales to pass the monotony and to explain the unease they felt at certain spots? Or did they actually see a strange old man who fascinated and yet terrified them who evolved into a hermit or wandering monk? What is significant to me is that my pendulum has demonstrated violent reactions in legendary spots *before* I have discovered any of the stories behind the places.

On the Trail of a Legend

The wanderings of the Hermit of Culver Cliff, a beauty spot on one of the southernmost tips of the Isle of Wight leys, are often fixed in the time of Edward III, a suitably distant period. In two of the spots where his presence was recorded, not only I but also my children who had no knowledge of the legend, commented on a sense of foreboding and experienced sudden flashes of inexplicable irritation and even anger, although on the surface both locations should have induced calm and pleasure.

The third spot, a lost village, is one that, at the time of writing, I am trying to pinpoint. The general area of this village is one in which, from my first days on the island, I felt ill at ease. All three places were along what I later found out to be a recognised ley and at one point a crossing point for two such lines.

The dark feelings occurred most strongly at this ley intersection near the huge, brightly painted statue of a pirate
outside the Blackgang Chine theme park on the western side
of the Isle of Wight, once the haunt of smugglers. I took the
pendulum to the spot between the giant pirate's feet and it
made large negative swings, although logically it should be a
joyous place with so many children visiting the fun park.

On exploring local folklore I discovered that virtually
where the plaster pirate stood, tales of another giant, the
giant of Chale, had grown up centuries before. His cave was
reputedly close to the present pleasure park. His wickedness
was well known, and a holy man, on deeper investigation
almost certainly the legendary Hermit of Culver Cliff, went
to the giant's lair to persuade the giant to change his evil
ways. The cave was full of hideous winged creatures and the
skulls of slain animals and people.

The giant would have killed the holy man but he made the
sign of the cross and cursed the land where the cave stood
saying that henceforward nothing should grow there and a
red stream should flow from that spot, filled with the giant's
blood. The holy man also prophesied that the coast would
crumble away.

For many years a red stream coursed down the cliff and
Blackgang Chine has been dramatically eroded, like much of
the West Wight Coastline. Although lovely flowers and trees
grow in the pleasure park where the children play, outside
the land is bleak and barren. The area above the park is
frequently shrouded in mist and anyone who peers through
the greyness can imagine the sad shadows of those lured by
the giant to his lair.

Dowsing for Legends

This can be a great activity if you go to a new area on holiday, or even for a day, and is a good way of beginning to dowse for ghosts because the legends told over centuries have kept the ghosts of the area alive and added the emotions of the tellers, so that there will be powerful markers. There may even be an amalgam of ghosts that have become enmeshed in the legend.

☆ Begin by locating a ruined abbey, an overgrown well or a long-abandoned castle; look on an Ordanance Survey map for a place with an unusual or evocative name.

☆ Visit the spot with your pendulum either in the early morning or evening when the vibes are least disturbed by present day visitors.

☆ Start walking with your pendulum on a straight line towards your focus, and on a scribbled sketch map mark any spots where the pendulum responds strongly either positively or negatively, for some places can reflect great joy, especially on a pilgrim trail to a sacred well.

☆ Even more importantly, stop at each point and close your eyes, letting any images or sounds form. Scribble them down, no matter how unlikely, together with key words about your own feelings.

☆ When you reach the ruin, let your pendulum again give you a response, and when you have noted this look all round and see if there are any significant markers: a huge rock on top of a hill or a distant church spire. It may be that buildings have obscured the landmarks, in which case return to your map and look for an aligned place with another inter-esting name and follow the direct route between the two as closely as possible.

☆ Keep making notes and let your pendulum guide you.

☆ When you have a number of 'sightings' – for you may even detect the faint glow of your legendary monk or king – go to the nearest town or tourist village and purchase a book of local legends.

☆ You will probably find that your trail evoked some of the story quite spontaneously, and if you later study the history of the location you may be able to identify events and personalities that gave rise to the stories.

Following a Ghost's Path

You are now ready to follow a specific ghost path, perhaps a rose walk in a stately home or the length of a long gallery or cathedral aisle where people walked while experiencing strong emotions.

☆ When trying to tune into ghosts, first walk up and down a straight natural pathway in an old house, cloisters or a garden where people would have paced up and down over time, lost in thought or trying to calm strong emotion and leaving a strong imprint. It is this residual feeling that your pendulum will detect and enable you to tread in the path of the past. Let your pendulum swing quite naturally vertically as you walk. If the path appears to be blocked, find a swirl of energy and ask the pendulum to indicate the path the phantom wants to travel.

☆ You may find that your pendulum swings a different way from the normal positive/negative circling that it used on the trail of legends, as the ghosts become more specific and personalised. It may form ellipses or even swing strongly from left to right or vibrate in the presence of the ghost.

☆ Do not study the history of the place until after your initial foray as this may colour your spontaneous impressions. Suddenly you may feel the hairs on the back of your neck tingling or a sudden drop in temperature as you come within the field of the ghost whose aura may extend several metres all round.

☆ Half close your eyes and look at the area surrounding the pendulum to see if a misty shape encloses it. Quartz crystal is especially good for amplifying ghost energy and you may see a momentary flash of light as you catch a brief picture of your ghost either externally or in your mind's eye.

☆ Move a few centimetres away and the reaction will cease, unless the presence is accompanying you in which case your pendulum will stay in positive mode and the vibrations will continue. If this occurs, you will wish to ask the ghost to leave you when you leave the site. Thank him or her for their company and wish them well but explain that you now wish to cease contact. At this point, put your pendulum away. Because the ghost is so attached to the place, it is unlikely that it would follow you but it is important to mark the beginning and end of paranormal contact so that your energies are not receptive to less benign influences.

☆ When you get home, cleanse and recharge your pendulum.

EXERCISE: PSYCHOMETRY WITH YOUR PENDULUM

Psychometry, the psychic art of touching to transmit information about the history of an artefact, is a gentle but effective way of contacting a ghost if the object is *in situ*. However, rather than touching the artefact, which can be difficult with delicate items, you can use your pendulum to dowse over an object in an old house or castle and through it feel by amplification the lives of the people connected with the sights, sounds and fragrances it evokes.

Indeed, I have found that the pendulum does magnify psychometric impressions; this is, from my own experience, the most effective way of seeing or sensing a ghost, especially if you have not had any success following a ghost path.

☆ Passing a pendulum around or over an object focuses your innate psychic abilities and can create in the mind's eye visual images or even words, fragrances and tastes, such as salt, tar or spices that are not present in the room.

☆ As with tracing a ghost path, your pendulum may respond to the psychic vibes with ellipses or a horizontal swing and vibration when it comes into contact with another dimension.

☆ Find artefacts that belong to the place or at the very least are of the correct period for the room in which they are displayed, as this will evoke the presence of a ghost who will have resonance with the object, especially if it has been in the house over many years.

☆ Visit a place such as an industrial museum where you can wander around on your own and where there are artefacts that you can get close to without adverse comment.

☆ If possible, try for a multi-sensory experience where there are fragrances, perhaps a vase of roses or a bowl of lavender that have been part of domestic life over many centuries and so span the dimensions. If not, carry your own lavender or rose spray or essential oil and sniff it before beginning dowsing.

☆ The sound of machinery or transport, though not a commentary, can also help to evoke the presence of the past – some museums are relaxed about allowing visitors to sit in reconstructed wartime shelters or on old buses so that you can feel and smell the rich leather seats.

☆ Hold your pendulum on a fairly short chain about 5cm (2in) from the artefact and let the pendulum move as it will. You are less concerned with the nature of the swing than with the feelings and senses it transmits. Crystal pendulums are the best type to hold over an object for psychometric purposes.

☆ Some people may feel cold spots when standing still with the pendulum at regular points throughout the building that may or may not correspond to a drop in physical temperature. This coldness can indicate the presence of an other-worldly or at least psychic force. It occurs when two dimensions meet and is not a sign of anything sinister.

☆ If this does occur, hold the pendulum over the nearest artefact and you may be rewarded by the sense of even the faint glow of a figure who is touching the object. Do not be afraid; you are seeing the image as on a television screen and it cannot hurt you, but if you do feel uneasy, move away. Thank the presence silently for revealing him- or herself. Alternatively, you may hear in your mind's ear a story unfolding about a person who loved the artefact.

8

Remote or Map Dowsing

Map or remote dowsing means dowsing at a distance from the actual target area, and is in many ways the most psychic aspect of pendulum work. Some people find the idea of remote or map dowsing slightly intimidating because they imagine it involves strict measurements with rulers, angles and complex calculations, but such dowsing can be of great value whether looking for ley lines, water, minerals or lost objects, as you can save a great deal of shoe leather and time by precisely locating an item from the comfort of your living room. Equally, if you are lost in a maze of country lanes without a sign post, or in the middle of a wood with no idea of the way back to the car, you can dowse over a scribbled diagram to show you the way, while if you have misplaced your car keys or your credit cards at home and are in a hurry, you can draw a plan of your house to narrow down your area of search to one corner of a specific room.

Remote mapping can be applied to almost every aspect of dowsing, many of which I have already touched on, albeit using different terminology. When choosing a holiday destination from an atlas or a new home in another part of town using a grid, you are in essence remote dowsing. If there is an absent loved one to whom you wish to send healing, you can dowse over a representation of the person's body to pinpoint the correct part of the body; you can even create a dream map to *find a way* through your dreams. So we have already moved far from grid references to areas where the dowsing is more important and therefore emotionally charged.

Map divination is akin to clairvoyance, which means 'clear seeing', and especially to remote viewing whereby a person can see the location of another person and what he or she is doing. Every time the pendulum is asked about a decision you are using exactly the same process as that employed in map divination, including visualisation. I actually find it easier to dowse at a distance rather than wandering round with a pendulum, especially if the place is in public and self-consciousness and fear of failure inhibit natural intuitions.

In chapter 4 you tried pendulum dowsing for a friend or family member by drawing a sketch map and pinpointing their movements, and this is a technique you can develop. All you need to do is concentrate on the location rather than the subject so that eventually you can link into distant locations and events without needing the focus of a person to act as a marker. At this point, getting lost or mislaying keys become problems of the past.

For some people, the more physical the dowsing, the less easy they find it and if your primary skills lie as a map dowser rather than in the field, utilise that aspect of your gift even when looking for water or minerals, so that when you go to a location you have a good idea where to look in advance and so avoid any initial panic that can block intuition. I have suggested books and organisations that will help if you are interested in developing more formal map dowsing skills (see Useful Addresses and Further Reading), but you can work quite informally, especially initially.

Tuning Into Your Clairvoyant Powers

Alfred Watkins, who first discovered ley lines when he was 65 years old and wrote *The Old Straight Track* in 1925, 'became aware of a network of lines – standing out like wires all over the surface of the countryside'. He perceived the existence of the ley system in a single flash as he was riding his horse across the hills near Bredwardine in his native Herefordshire, and suddenly saw a network of tracks intersecting at the sites of churches, crosses, old stones and other sanctified sites. Watkins was not a mystic, however, but a merchant, archaeologist, photographer and inventor. I would argue that this same holistic vision is utilised by the best dowsers, who see not lines and grid references on paper, but rushing streams, sunlit hillsides and ancient outcrops on the tops of hills.

☆ Begin with an area you know and love.

☆ Pass your pendulum over a map and ask it to make a positive response at your favourite place.

☆ It is helpful if all your senses are involved in building up a clear inner image of the distant spot; hear the song of the birds or the roar of the traffic, smell the roses or spices, and even taste the salt of the sea or wood smoke.

The Time and the Place

In chapter 4 you practised targeting friends and family at certain times by focusing on the people themselves. Now you are going to change the lens on the psychic camera and, using your pendulum and a map, concentrate on bringing the places into sharp focus.

☆ If you have friends or family members who are going on a touring holiday even for a weekend, ask them to keep a note of places visited, the route taken and timings.

☆ Use as large a scale map as possible of the planned trip.

☆ At different times each day, pass your pendulum over villages, towns and roads, asking it to give you a positive response when you link in with your friends.

☆ When this occurs, try to tune into a key location using the multi-sensory approach.

☆ In the evening, sit down with the map and ask your pendulum to show you the entire route taken that day and the subjects' current location if they are staying in different places each night.

☆ At each location identified on the map by the pendulum, evoke as many images as you can: the donkey with the hat that was eating the flower beds next to the fountain in the dusty square, the sudden shrill of a flock of migrating birds.

☆ Do not use logic or try to second-guess. People rarely keep to recommended routes.

☆ Timescales are not a problem as your pendulum operates outside chronological measurements, although it will always work best for a current situation or location. You can therefore calculate not only where your subjects *are* at a certain time, but where they *were* 12 hours earlier. The only proviso is that you set the parameters of time for your pendulum as it is passing over the map, for example 'Show me where Lynne and Dave were at 2 p.m. today' (remember to allow for any time zone differences) and recreate the moment as though you are stepping into a time capsule to the past, which thereby becomes the present.

☆ On return, check the subjects' notes and see how many hits you scored. Keep trying at every opportunity as visualisation of location is the key to all forms of remote dowsing.

Finding Your Way with the Pendulum

You go out for a walk in the forest having parked your car and become thoroughly lost; or you miss your turn on a slip road, perhaps while driving in a foreign country or by a series of unwelcome diversion signs, and have no idea where you are. None of the local places on the sign post feature on your map, it is getting dark and you are tired. No-one is in the mood to follow a pendulum. You need to find where the car is now and to plot a series of stages to confirm that you are getting nearer. This technique will work if you believe it will work – I can find my way in strange towns if I do not think about it or try to be logical. Trust yourself. If you become lost while walking, the following steps may help you to get back on track. The method can be adapted for driving:

☆ Draw a rough plan, marking where *you* are in the middle of the paper with a cross.

☆ Include any immediate features such as a stream, and orient these by either the sun or your compass if you have it.

☆ Failing that, ask your pendulum: 'Do I need to cross the stream/climb the hill to return to my car by the most direct currently accessible route?'

☆ The reference to the direct currently accessible route means you will avoid boggy ground and returning by the circuitous route by which you came.

☆ If you are surrounded by trees and there is no sun or moon, use the pendulum alone to orient yourself. After all, even if you knew where north was, by now you may have no real idea if you have walked in a circle.

☆ Now define your ultimate destination of this journey to the pendulum: 'I want to find my green car in the car park next to the Park Forest Visitors' Centre where we left it to begin this walk. Show me this place on the map so that where I am standing now is facing towards the car.'

☆ Beginning in the top left corner, work your way along the edges of the paper until the pendulum circles positively somewhere on one of the four edges to show where the car is.

☆ Mark this with a cross, but do not join the two points, except with a dotted line, as the route may have many twists and turns.

☆ The next question is: 'How far is it in metres by the nearest most accessible route to the car from where I am now, accepting that each number on the map represents 10 metres?'

☆ Write a number square 1–100 in the opposite corner of the map and dowse over it. So now you know the worst or may be pleasantly surprised; at least you can now break the journey down into manageable stages.

☆ It is unlikely that you will be able to reach the car by walking in a straight line, so ask the pendulum to show you on the sketch map by the direction of its swing the direction you should take to the first distinguishing feature you will see on the return route, at which you need to change direction.

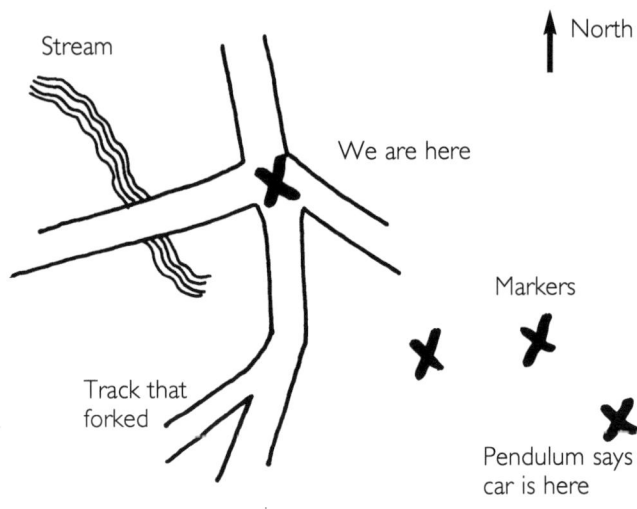

A rough plan showing how to find your way with a pendulum

☆ If you are still on a path this may involve making a right-angle turn, but even through forest there is usually a network of tracks.

☆ Back to the number chart: 'In how many metres will this change of direction occur?' Mark this spot on the sketch with a cross at approximately the right distance from where you are now.

☆ Using the visualisation technique, focus on the first cross on your way and allow a picture to build up in your mind of what you will find there, maybe a whole clearing of wild bluebells or a tree with the face of a witch. If this is not initially the way you came, you may join up with your original route nearer the destination.

☆ When you have reached this spot, using your pendulum as a guide, you need to repeat the whole process starting from marking a cross to denote your present location so that you can mark the next stage of the journey, again with rough distances.

☆ If there is an intersection of tracks, draw these on the map and dowse over them for the correct one. Continue to mark your map with crosses until you have drawn out the entire route, but only visualise one place at a time as you reach the previous mental marker point.

☆ Anticipate the pleasure and relief you will feel when you see the car again as though it were happening right now.

☆ As you get nearer your destination, you can mark off your crosses on the map. But once you do recognise familiar landmarks do not abandon your pendulum mapping entirely until the car is in sight. After all, logic got you lost in the first place.

☆ As you get nearer your goal your visualisations will get even stronger.

Grid Dowsing

A good method for isolating a small relevant area is to overlay a map or chart with a grid, dividing it into squares. Draw the grid on tracing paper if you wish to avoid marking the printed plan; the area covered can be any size, the principle is the same.

☆ If you wish you can number the grid or use normal map grid markings, creating on your own charts a scale to suit the area if necessary.

☆ Hold your pendulum over each grid in turn as you did when dowsing for decisions and ask the pendulum either to make a positive response or to pull down and vibrate over the square that contains whatever it is you are seeking.

☆ If there are a number of items close together to be located, for example converging water veins, you can ask: 'Is there more than one water vein in this square/more than two/more than three?'

☆ If the area is too large to easily dowse, you can further narrow the search by either changing to a map that is on a larger scale, or by sub-dividing the target square into smaller squares and dowsing over each one with your pendulum.

Map Dowsing Using Co-ordinates

☆ Hold your pendulum at one corner of the map and as you move your pendulum slowly from east to west, ask it to indicate the direction of your search object along the edge of the map by making a positive circle.

☆ Tell the pendulum to make an ellipse just before the point and a reverse ellipse when you have passed the point so that you can mark the exact spot along the line (Point 1 on the diagram overleaf).

☆ Now ask your pendulum to indicate by its swing the angle of the line, as you did when you were trying to find a destination when you were lost. Draw a dotted line along this angle of swing. Follow the direction of the pendulum until it spins. That is the end of your first line.

☆ Now ask the pendulum to select a second marker point along the north/south (left) edge of the map, as shown in the diagram (Point 2). Other practitioners draw two points along the east/west bottom edge of the map, at positions indicated by the pendulum and then direct angles of swing from those. It does not matter which you use in what is sometimes called the triangulation method.

☆ Again ask the pendulum to indicate the angle of swing and draw another dotted line on the map until it spins to tell you to stop.

☆ Where your two lines meet will give you the apex of the triangle and your location point (Point 3). If your pendulum does not spin to indicate the end of the line, it does

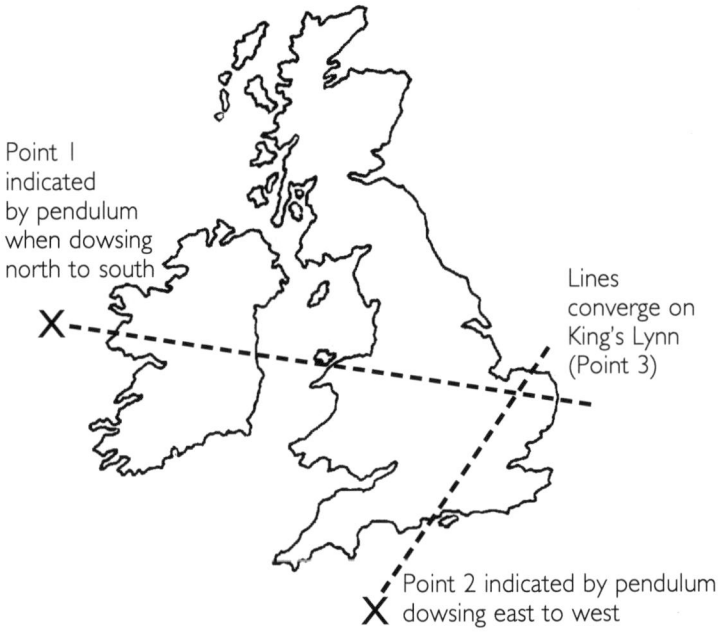

Point 1 indicated by pendulum when dowsing north to south

Lines converge on King's Lynn (Point 3)

X

Point 2 indicated by pendulum dowsing east to west
X

Using map dowsing to locate a suitable holiday cottage location

not matter, as the line angles of the lines from Points 1 and 2 will automatically intersect at the right point.

EXERCISE: MAP DOWSING

To test this method, you do not need a formal map, but can choose a large area of sand or earth and ask a friend to bury an object in the ground.

☆ Use the triangulation method to locate the item on a sketch and then take your pendulum and dowse for the object by walking along one of the lines on the ground in the area indicated, at the precise angle shown on the map.

☆ Ask a friend to walk along the second line at the same time at the precise angle indicated and you will meet.

☆ If you ask your pendulums to make an ellipse just before the object and a circle when it is over it, your pendulums should circle in the same place.

☆ You do not need a second person if you have the map, but it is good to see the effects *in situ*.

☆ If the area covered is vast, you will need to make smaller triangles within the original one by dowsing along the base of the triangle for two further points and angles of swing.

☆ If the area is small, another method is to start from a single point, moving your pendulum along the line of swing; as it approaches the item it will start to make an ellipse, then a circle when it is over the item, reverting to an ellipse as the item is passed. This is not as accurate as triangulation, however.

☆ If you are seeking a single item on a formal map, you can use the co-ordinates marked along the edge of the map, holding a pencil in one hand and your pendulum in the other.

☆ Point with the pencil to each of the co-ordinates in turn starting at the left-hand edge along the horizontal side, and ask your pendulum to make a positive circle if the item is at that co-ordinate mark this with a dot.

☆ Then travel up the vertical left-hand side with your pencil, again asking the pendulum to indicate the correct co-ordinate. Mark with another dot. Draw lines with a ruler and where they meet is the correct spot. You can also use this for representations using graph paper.

EXERCISE: DOWSING YOUR DREAMS – CREATING A 'DREAMOGRAM'

Too frequently we wake from a dream at the moment at which we are about to discover the answer to a problem or a new insight into our lives. Even if we can return to the dream, the spontaneity may be gone. I first used 'dreamograms' as a simple device for recalling and developing dreams for healing, but it is also a valuable way of developing dream material during waking hours, and the pendulum offers access to the deep unconscious wisdom from which the dream derived.

☆ Begin with a dream, a particularly vivid recurring dream, and write it down, seeing it as you would with a painting or poem as a series of images.

☆ If you find it difficult to recall your dreams, keep a notebook by your bed for a few days and jot down notes the minute you wake, even if this is the middle of the night. This helps you to build up dream recall.

☆ Taking each major image of your chosen recurring dream, on a separate sheet of paper write or draw a symbol to represent it. You may use one word or several.

☆ Dowse over this representation with your pendulum as you did on your map when trying to connect with friends on holiday, visualising each image in all its aspects – sounds, smells and even tastes – until ideas start to flow.

☆ Use your pendulum to clarify ideas by asking yes/no questions, so filling in the elusive missing pieces.

☆ Write these associated ideas as spokes radiating from the main symbol. These ideas encapsulate what each symbol means to you. Do not use any dream dictionaries, but rely on your own definitions, especially in the context of the dream. Some ideas may evoke strong emotions. Draw a circle to enclose your word wheel.

☆ Do this with each symbol in the dream, until you have a series of unconnected dream wheels.

☆ After you have completed the wheels, place the separate papers in a honeycomb formation.

☆ Begin by passing your pendulum over the whole honeycomb from the top left-hand corner, asking your pendulum to indicate by a positive response over the correct order of symbols the route through the dream, so that symbol one may be followed by symbol five, rather than the order in which you recalled them. If necessary, rearrange the wheels.

☆ Draw in connection lines between the wheels so that you have an interconnected honeycomb. Look at your honeycomb during the day, but do not attempt to analyse it.

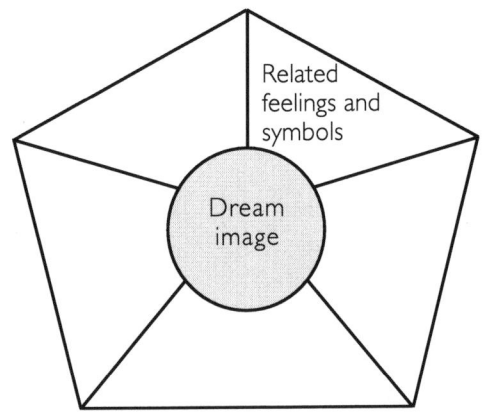

A dreamogram

☆ When you have a quiet moment during the evening, light a pink or lilac candle and study your dreamogram, asking your pendulum to point out any significant additional markers on the way.

☆ Your dream now forms a coherent story.

☆ Sit in the candle light and continue the story from where the dream left off, allowing your inner voice to dictate the events and resolution. At each stage ask the pendulum if that is the next stage and if it gives a negative response, relax and let another scenario replace the first.

☆ When the pendulum confirms that you have found the true resolution, you will understand the relevance of the original dream to your current situation.

9

Physical
Dowsing

This final chapter of the book looks at dowsing at its most physical and demonstrable. You should now have the confidence to go into the field and apply your intuitive skills to the material world. For some people, physical dowsing is less important than dowsing for decisions or for health-related matters; they argue that in their current environment it is unlikely that will ever need to find a place to dig a well and it is a view that to some extent I share. But I would say that there are many situations in which it is useful to be able to find a leak in an underground pipe so that you can direct professional repairers, or if you are skilled in DIY, cut down on hours of searching by conventional methods.

Yet most people still associate physical dowsing with rows of dowsers trying to find water under test conditions. If you enjoy tests it can be great fun, for water dowsing is perhaps the most ancient psychic art and still the most useful given the universal need for clean drinking water. The United Nations has estimated that about two billion people world-wide lack high-quality drinking water and this number increases every year – so maybe it is worth developing your expertise.

There are many forms of physical dowsing, but they all follow the same method. Whether you are looking for oil, metals, electricity or even buried treasure, you can programme your pendulum to discriminate between different underground substances by carefully defining the parameters of your search. While mineral and water dowsers do incorporate map dowsing to narrow down the necessity of searching a wide area on foot, every would-be dowser should attempt physical dowsing, if only to confirm the accuracy of map dowsing – and their internal intuitive processes.

Water dowsing is also a particularly good way of tuning into the energies of the earth. Because so much of our bodies is made up of fluid, we have great kinship with water – witness the emotions experienced when walking by the sea. Water dowsing is especially easy in the weeks of the new and full moon which also have the most dramatic effect on the tides. So if you found earth energy dowsing difficult, you may find that actually dowsing for a specific dome of water or intersection without trying to tune into the past, does open up the whole field for you.

Though you may never be asked to locate a site for a well, it can be very useful to be able to trace an oil leak on your car, locate hazardous wiring inside a wall, or find out whether a source of drinking water is pure. Let me give you a practical example taken from a newspaper of how physical dowsing can help in everyday life. In July 1999, David Moore, who farms near Torrington in Devon, could not understand his cows' reluctance to enter the milking parlour. Mr Moore asked the advice of fellow farmer, Cyril Cole, who was also an expert dowser. With a hazel rod, Mr Cole detected a tiny leak of electricity in a cable running below the ground where the cows had to walk. By switching off the supply on that circuit Mr Moore was able to milk his Friesians without difficulty.

The Scientific Evidence for Physical Dowsing

Professor Hans-Dieter Betz, a physicist at the University of Munich, undertook a ten-year programme sponsored by the German government, applying dowsing methods for water sources in arid areas including Sri Lanka, Zaire, Kenya, Namibia and Yemen. The results indicated overwhelming evidence for the existence of dowsing abilities. Dowsers attained an overall success rate of 96 per cent in 691 drillings in Sri Lanka, as against the estimated success rate of 30–50 per cent expected by conventional methods in an area where finding water purely by chance was extremely unlikely. Professor Betz's most plausible hypothesis was that subtle electromagnetic gradients resulting from the fissures and water flows created changes in the electrical properties of rock and soil, and that dowsers sensed these gradients in what was described as a 'hypersensitive state'.

So the psychic element exists even here. Such a hypothesis would not explain map dowsing abilities, but it may be that as with other psychic arts different abilities come to the fore according to the nature of the quest.

As discussed in chapter 1, dowsing is increasingly used by both the military and businesses. Dr Peter Treadwell, former vitamin-plant director for Hoffman-La Roche, the multinational pharmaceutical firm based in Basle, Switzerland, was sent all over the world to dowse water for his company's prospective factory sites. Dr Treadwell commented: 'The plain truth is that we keep finding water for our company with a method that neither physics nor physiology nor psychology has even begun to explain. Roche uses methods that are profitable whether they are scientifically explainable or not. The dowsing method pays off. It is 100 percent reliable.'

Beginning Physical Dowsing

The first thing to remember is that physical dowsing is fun, not a test of your abilities, unless at some stage you do join a dowsing organisation and decide to take part in some of their organised activities and learn from experts the tips they have picked up over the years. You can dowse for water or other substances on days out or whenever you have a desire or need. As with any new skill, begin with a known source of surface water so that you and your pendulum establish meaningful communication that you can utilise when you are searching for an unknown source.

Using Natural Clues

When you do start to look for underground water it is not cheating to use, as do all creatures, natural clues to supplement intuition.

In chapter 6, I mentioned cats that sleep in positive energy spots and that domes of water or at least sacred veins are a feature of sacred sites. So you can be sure that where your cat – or even better a neighbourhood stray that is more closely linked with the great outdoors – regularly sleeps over a place where veins of water cross, you should dowse there. Foxes, badgers, and the famous US groundhog that foretells the weather on 2 February, invariably have underground veins of water close to the entrances of their setts. Deer too settle for the night over the crossing of veins of water, and if you are not squeamish a large anthill is also a good indicator. Your pendulum may spin clockwise due to the force of the intersecting waters, especially at ancient sites where a ley line may bisect the crossing. But if you ask your pendulum just to follow one vein of water, it will do so (see the exercise later in this chapter).

If there is a tree in a clearing that has all its greenery on one side and has not been struck by lightning or uprooted, the branches will be leaning towards an underground source of water; apple and maple trees may assume a corkscrew formation. The cedar is another very water-sensitive tree and will grow in a circle round a dome of water.

I have already mentioned standing stones, but the ultimate indicator of water is a holy well. This will be fed from a sacred stream that may be entirely submerged. Or you may have to look for the holy well itself if it is disused, using your water dowsing skills. Find place names such as Bridewell, Holywell, Nunwell or Ladywell, and you are in a good spot for water dowsing and may discover a neglected or abandoned sacred source of water that will also abound with ley energies.

Crypts of churches and cathedrals built on ancient temple sites may also conceal an old well or spring. At Chartres Cathedral in France, for example, the old well behind the cathedral was probably used by the druids. The early Celtic Christian church used these former pagan wells for baptism until the Roman church replaced them with the font inside the building.

Using Visualisation

As with other forms of dowsing, if you can *see* with your inner eye what you are seeking, you will be better able to find it in actuality. Veins of water flow through the earth at various levels and are very common in fertile regions, although the water may not be suitable for drinking purposes.

☆ If you are unfamiliar with geology you may find it helpful to read a basic illustrated book about the earth's crust, and also visit either a geological museum or this section of your local museum. The Natural History Museum in South Kensington in London offers a hands-on experience with beautiful displays and videos so that you can see externally how different soils create different kinds and depths of flow, so that for example with clay soil, water will flow across or beneath it but not through the clay itself.

☆ When you begin, find a location where there is a river, a natural lake or pond.

☆ Picture the piece of land on which you are standing as part of a huge body, with underground veins of water connecting different parts, breaking through fissures in the rock, flowing and pulsating through arteries and sometimes rising as a stream to feed a sacred well. In earlier times, ancient peoples believed the well was the entrance to the Earth Mother's womb.

☆ See the subterranean water courses tinged different colours from the earth, a beautiful rainbow of yellows, browns and reds, passing through glints of quartz, then flowing clear as they increase in intensity, break free of their bonds and merge perhaps miles away to join with a mighty river and become part of the ocean.

☆ Connect with the pulse of the earth, putting your ear to the ground and *hearing* the regular beat. This stage is well worth developing as you can link in with the physical substance using the homing device of the water within you. Now allow the background of earth to fade and the water veins to come into sharp focus.

☆ Hold your pendulum over the ground and ask it to indicate by its positive response when it is over water, any water, and as your pendulum moves, which it will do, do not worry about following the flow but let the vibration of the underground vein find resonance in the fluid that flows within you. I have described the damp, cold feeling that you experience when close to water; it is almost as if your body becomes an extension of the pendulum when connection is made.

You are now a bona fide water diviner or water witch and your next task, if you wish, is to refine the technique so that you can discriminate between different veins of water, discover what is suitable drinking water, and identify other underground substances, pipes, electricity cables, metals and even oil, though you are more likely to discover a buried oil drum than make your fortune by striking oil.

Veins of water are generally about 7cm (3in) wide, with the greatest power of attraction at the centre of the channel, although they can be up to 15cm (6in). The aura of the water may extend beyond this so dowse for the centre where the response is strongest. They will be at different depths and flow at varying rates, but you can ascertain these factors using your pendulum once you have practised the basic techniques for a little longer.

Going With the Flow

You have felt the *water* response so the next stage is to begin isolating specific veins of water and then to explore depth and the capacity of flow.

☆ Begin this time from a surface source of water – a stream, river or even natural pond – and work backwards.

☆ Look for feeder brooks which flow into the main body of water. In dry weather when the water level is low, these can be seen as cracks just above the water line.

☆ Look for small 2.5–5cm (1–2in) wide veins flowing from the banks and choose one.

☆ Ask your pendulum to: 'Give me the track of the vein of water I chose which I will name A.'

☆ You may find it helps to call the separate veins A, B, C, etc. to avoid ambiguity when talking to the pendulum. With your pendulum, walk parallel but fairly close to the stream, upstream from the way it is flowing. At some point you will cut across Vein A and you will get a reaction. Mark the spot with a peg (tent pegs are ideal). If you had asked for all water you would have encountered several crossing points.

☆ Keep a blank mind and do not try to guess or analyse the logical flow of the water underground, which may be at right angles to the stream, remain roughly parallel or waver.

☆ Walk over the whole area beyond your marker, keeping the stream in sight, following a snake-like curve so that you cover the whole area. It may help to envisage the area divided into squares. Ask your pendulum to identify only the course of the original vein you selected on the bank.

☆ Now ask the pendulum to identify another vein of water which you call B. Again, mark the places where your pendulum responds and if you push in pegs, you see quite clearly the course of B. As you expand the area of search you may discover more veins and be rewarded by your pendulum spinning clockwise where a number meet.

☆ Another useful skill to cultivate is finding the direction of a stream which is not evident in underground streams that may be too deep to surface into the visible stream or pond.

Discovering Direction and Depth

☆ Pick the peg most distant from the stream and ask the pendulum if this is the 'down flow'.

☆ Continue to ask at each marker point until you can plot the way the vein is flowing. This is a useful skill, as you do not want your vein flowing under a sewage bed or other pollution if it is being directed into a well or into a stream used for drinking.

☆ You may find that this second vein does not surface at the stream where you began. In this case there are no feeder marks, and when you dowse, you will observe that the vein veers off in a different direction.

☆ The next skill to practise is to find the depth of the chosen vein.

☆ Use your quantity/intensity circle from chapter 2 and ask the pendulum to indicate by either the positive response or by tugging down, using each number to represent the nearest 3m (10ft) to the actual depth.

I have deliberately not explored the issue of whether water is safe for drinking here as you need to be confident at finding water before you impose further conditions upon your investigations.

Measuring the Flow

You do not need to assess the rate of flow unless you are trying to find a place for a well, but it is a good technique to practise to build up your picture of the water which you are dowsing and so become more generally tuned in to different kinds and veins of water. A good method to use is your quantity/intensity circle chart and ask the pendulum to tell you how many litres a minute are flowing at this time through the vein. A small vein may yield as little as a litre a minute.

Is This Water Safe for Drinking?

What matters from a practical point of view is whether water, either on the surface or from an underground source, is safe to drink. If you are hill-walking or camping you may need to replenish a water bottle from a stream; while travelling you may see a drinking fountain in a square and wonder if it really is drinkable; or if you are in a different country you may be uncertain whether tap water is suitable to drink, clean your teeth or wash fruit and salad. Even if you live in an urban area, your water supply may not be entirely free from harmful substances and this has been the cause of a great deal of controversy in recent years. If you are buying a house or apartment, the piping may be very old and still contain lead.

Whatever the situation the method is the same, whether the water can be seen or not. Ask your pendulum, not is this water *pure*, for few sources are, but *is it safe to drink?* If the pendulum circles only slowly, ask the pendulum how safe on a scale of ten. Try the water that comes out of your household cold water tap. If the pendulum gives a negative reaction, dowse your domestic pipes as far as the road and see whether your pipes are causing problems – perhaps they need replacing – or if the problem lies with the Water Board.

Remember, if you are dowsing in a stream and are upstream, ask your pendulum about the quality of water at regular intervals further downstream, in case it has been polluted by animals.

Is This Water Safe to Bathe in?

River, lake and ocean pollution is a major environmental crisis, and even beaches that have been awarded a water safety certificate can become polluted between tests. Different countries also have different standards and stringencies with which national and international recommendations are implemented.

Before you swim, take some water from the lake or sea in a clear tumbler and hold your pendulum over it. Ask your pendulum if the water is safe for you to swim in – and if you have children ask again for them as they may be more susceptible to infection.

Dowsing for Oil and Minerals

Dr Alexander K. Bakirov, professor of geology and mineralogy at the Tomsk Polytechnical Institute in Siberia, is one of several several dozen Russian specialists charged with locating new natural resources in his country. 'Dowsing', Dr Bakirov has written, 'is being used in my country to solve geological problems in the location of gold sulfides, copper-molybdenum, tin-tungsten, rare-metal and many other ores.' He cites the successful location by dowsing of industrially important mineral deposits in the Yenisei Mountains after normal geological prospecting had failed to find any ore over a period of many years. During a helicopter flight, spots were also dowsed from the air where soil erosion was threatening to crack a 400km gas pipe running from Ukhta to Torzhok.

I said earlier that if you divine for oil you are more likely to unearth a disused oil drum than black gold. However, you may be like Paul Clement Brown of California, who for years advised one of America's most successful petroleum 'wildcatters', J.K. Wadley, on whether or not his proposed oil-drilling sites would be productive and how deep the oil would lie. Brown's main device was a hand-held pendulum. His ability to dowse for oil was tested by an initially sceptical senior petroleum engineer, Chet Davis, on 35 proposed well sites. 'He was right on all 35 wells,' says Davis. 'I don't think anyone in the oil business would believe it if they didn't see it. I wouldn't have.'

A Home Test

When dowsing for water, I always specifically ask my pendulum to find *only water*, thereby excluding electricity cables and so on. However, some dowsers argue that a pendulum or for that matter any other dowsing device, will automatically respond to any underground water, oil and minerals and that with practice you learn to discriminate what the pendulum is indicating.

You can test this for yourself at home and if you do find different reactions for substances, this can help to fine tune your dowsing so that although you are looking for water, you note that there is also an electricity cable close by or a metal pipe encasing the water. In time, you do become far more instinctive and ask fewer questions until at some point you may no longer need the pendulum or any other dowsing instrument, although you may always prefer to use one as confirmation of your intuition. This test can be attempted with a friend, perhaps taking it in turns to carry out the experiment.

☆ You will need five or more identical plastic opaque jars with lids.

☆ Put water in one jar, oil in another, copper discs in the third, iron nails in the fourth and some silver items in the fifth. If you have two or three gold rings or earrings, add these to a sixth jar and, if you wish, pure tin in a seventh. You can obtain tin coins from a museum.

☆ Make sure any metals are pure, as alloys may confuse the pendulum.

☆ Go out of the room while your friend arranges the jars in a row.

☆ Stand in front of the jars and say to your pendulum: 'I want you to ignore the container material entirely and react only to the contents of each.'

☆ Hold your pendulum over each jar in turn and let your mind go blank. Do not try to guess what is inside or in this experiment to 'see' psychically, but note the reaction of the pendulum over each and write it down, for example Jar 1 – an ellipse, Jar 2 – a double circle.

☆ It may give the same positive circling reaction for each. Do not worry, as you can question your pendulum to obtain the information. But try this periodically and you may find subtle differences in responses do emerge.

☆ Next hold your pendulum in front of the jars and ask it to: 'Show me with your positive circling by pulling down over the container with water/oil/inside' and pass the pendulum slowly over each container in turn. Do not try to guess. Note each.

☆ Look in the containers. If you were not right, remember this is a very artificial situation and most tests unconsciously increase anxiety, thereby increasing the likelihood of failure. The important thing is that you have started to investigate the different responses.

☆ Once you are looking for water, you will, with practice, automatically distinguish between water and other cables beneath the ground and if you dowse frequently in the city, even come to distinguish between a water as opposed to a gas pipe just by the swing of your pendulum.

☆ What is more, when dowsing on the beach or in a field, you will be able to tell when you have come to a ring-can-pull and when a treasure trove, and so may find dowsing with your psychic metal detector lucrative.

DIY With Your Pendulum

You can use your pendulum to detect almost any kind of fault if you specify what you are looking for. Even when you are working by psychic means, it is important to follow normal safety rules, however, especially if you are seeking an electricity cable. Metal pendulums can be lethal if they inadvertently come into contact with a live cable.

If you are looking for a leaking water pipe, ask your pendulum to react only to the stated substance, for example dripping water underground or in a wall. Once you have identified a drainage pipe, for example, you can track it over a distance of its course by moving along sideways facing it, checking with your pendulum at regular intervals that you are on course. Alternatively, if it is underground, place your body directly over the line and walk along its path, remembering that the point where you will find the leak or fractured pipe will be over your hands, not your feet.

You can also use the pendulum to detect problems with your car by asking it to detect a loose connection or an oil leak that defies a visual inspection. Given the high cost of car repairs, a preliminary dowse over your engine may also narrow down the cause of a problem, astounding mechanics who invariably ask 'What's the trouble then?'

☆ Break down the search into a series of subsequent stages that when you put the information together will give you an overall picture, for example, the far left-hand-nut on the fan belt is in fact loose, but the almost imperceptible oil dripping from the fifth connection to the right of the carburettor is also contributing to the overheating/lack of power.

☆ Open your bonnet and first ask your pendulum to identify any oil leaks that were causing problems the last time you used the car, by a positive response. This eliminates any future difficulties that may arise.

☆ Pass your pendulum slowly over each part of the engine in turn. Ask it to make a positive ellipse to mark the beginning of the problem and a negative ellipse to mark where the trouble ends.

☆ Scribble this down on a diagram and then ask the pendulum to indicate any electrical faults. This may be experienced as a buzzing in your hands even though the engine is switched off.

☆ Ask next about water and finally about any metal that is causing problems, either because it is too tight or loose or has become corroded inside.

☆ You can apply the same method to any faulty machinery.

☆ Just for fun, before you take a car in for a routine service or a safety certificate, run your pendulum over the whole car, including the tyres. You may be surprised how accurate you were in detecting faults, and if your mechanic does uncover others that were not borne out by your own experience of driving the vehicle, you can ask very politely whether these are essential repairs or potential faults that may need fixing in a month or so.

EXERCISE: IMPROVING THE QUALITY OF WATER

Even water that is safe to drink has all kinds of additives and minerals that may not suit your particular bodily make-up. Water filters do not solve all the problems and some people fear they remove nutrients in the form of salts and minerals.

☆ Early in the morning, run a clear jug of water from your tap.

☆ Place a large pure quartz crystal in the jug.

☆ Hold your pendulum over the jug and ask that everything in the water that is harmful in any way to your well-being is replaced by light and energy.

☆ Slowly circle your pendulum anti-clockwise nine times to remove negativity and then nine times clockwise to add energy.

☆ Cover the top of the jug and leave it until dusk in natural light, if possible outdoors close to trees and flowers or near an open window.

☆ You can also place the psychically cleansed water under a squat-shaped pyramid of glass, the true pyramid shape or even the frame of a pyramid. Tests have shown that pyramid water not only tastes better to drink, but alleviates headaches, bites and indigestion.

☆ Alternatively, if you drink bottled water, you will find a bewildering array on sale, each with subtly different compositions. Buy small bottles of a number of brands and ask your pendulum to indicate by circling or pulling down which is the best kind for you to help keep you healthy.

Further Reading

Dowsing

Bird, Christopher, *Divining*, Raven, Macdonald, 1979

Graves, Tom and Hoult, Janet, *The Essential T.C. Lethbridge*, Granada, 1982

Graves, Tom, *The Elements of Pendulum Dowsing*, Element, 1983

Lonegren, Sig, *Spiritual Dowsing*, Gothic Images, 1986

Background Reading

Andrews, Ted, *How to See and Read the Aura*, Llewellyn Publications, 1994

Bentov, Itzhak, *Stalking the Wild Pendulum: On the Mechanics of Consciousness*, Destiny Books, 1988

Tansley, David V., *Radionics: Science or Magic*, C.W. Daniel and Co., 1982

Tompkins, Peter and Bird, Christopher, *The Secret Life of Plants*, Harper & Row Publishers, 1973

Earth Energies and Ley Lines

Devereux, Paul, *Earth Mysteries: A Piatkus Guide*, Piatkus, 1999

Devereux, Paul, *Shamanism and the Mystery Lines*, Quantum, 1995

Heselton, Philip, *The Elements of Earth Mysteries*, Element, 1991

Palmer, Martin and Palmer, Nigel, *Sacred Britain*, Piatkus, 1999

Sullivan, Danny, *Ley Lines*, Piatkus, 1999

Watkins, Alfred, *The Old Straight Track*, Abacus, 1974

Wilson, Colin, *The Atlas of Holy Places and Sacred Sites*, Dorling Kindersley, 1996

Ghosts

Eason, Cassandra, *Ghost Encounters*, Blandford, 1997

Healing Energies

Bailey, Arthur, *Dowsing for Health*, Quantum, 1993

Barnard, Julian, *A Guide to the Bach Flower Remedies*, C.W. Daniel and Co., 1995

Eden, Donna, *Energy Medicine*, Piatkus, 1999

Kapchuk, Ted, *Chinese Medicine*, Century Books, 1987

Ozaniec, Naomi, *Elements of the Chakras*, Element, 1989

Wildwood, Chrissie, *The Encyclopedia of Healing Plants*, Piatkus, 1999

Visualisation

Graham, Helen, *Visualisation, An Introductory Guide*, Piatkus, 1996

Index

About the Author

Cassandra Eason is an international author, broadcaster and psychic consultant. She teaches psychic development and divination skills and has written 25 books on the paranormal, magic and divination, spiritual and religious experiences, and is an expert on folklore and superstition. She has also studied the history, psychology and esoteric practices of the Tarot for many years and given readings on radio and television programmes around the world.